Italian translation by
Eugenia de Stefani

Italian Phrase Book

Edmund Swinglehurst

NEWNES·BOOKS

First published in 1979 by
The Hamlyn Publishing Group Limited
Published in 1983 by Newnes Books,
Michelin House, 81 Fulham Road,
London SW3 6RB

Reprinted in 1992

ISBN 0 600 34900 4

Printed at Thomson Press (India) Ltd.
Faridabad (Haryana)

Contents

Contents

Introduction

The Newnes Italian Phrase Book is designed to help the reader who has no previous knowledge of the language. With its aid he should be able to make himself readily understood on all occasions and to cope with the host of minor problems – and some major ones – that can arise when on holiday or travelling in Italy.

The key to successful speech in a foreign language is pronunciation, and an outline of the principles of vowel and consonant sounds and their usage in Italian is to be found at the beginning of this book. This is followed by a section dealing with the essential elements of Italian grammar. A close study of these two sections and constant reference to them will be of the utmost value: with the pattern of sentence construction in mind and a feeling for the sound of the language, the reader will be well equipped to use the phrases in this book.

These are set out in logical order, beginning with the various means of travel and entry to the country. The section on accommodation covers the whole range from hotels and private houses and villas to youth hostels and camping sites. Particular attention is paid in the chapter on eating and drinking to the speciality dishes of Italian pasta and the many different kinds of Italian wines. Shopping, too, is covered in detail; whether the reader wishes to buy a pair of the famous Italian shoes or equip his self-catering apartment with a week's supply of groceries, he will find a selection of appropriate phrases easy to refer to and simple to use.

Entertainment, sightseeing, public services, and general conversations in the hotel bar are all covered, and there is an important section of commercial and banking phrases of particular value to the businessman. In addition to carefully chosen phrases, each section includes an appropriate vocabulary which is as comprehensive as possible, and at the end of the book there are quick-reference metric conversion tables for the more important temperatures, weights and measures.

The Newnes Italian Phrase Book will not only enable the traveller to handle any situation with confidence but will help to make his stay in Italy a more enjoyable one.

Guide to Italian Pronunciation

This is intended for people with no previous knowledge of Italian and is based on English pronunciation. This means that it is not entirely accurate but the reader who pays careful attention to this section should, with practice, be able to make himself understood reasonably well in Italian.

The Vowels

LETTER	APPROXIMATE PRONUNCIATION	EXAMPLE
a	like *a* in rather	**andare**
e	1 like *ay* in say	**sera**
	2 like *e* in met	**sette**
i	like *ee* in seen	**vino**
o	1 like *o* in over	**sole**
	2 like *o* in got	**notte**
u	1 like *oo* in soon	**luna**
	2 unstressed before another vowel, like *w* in water	**guida**

The Consonants

LETTER	APPROXIMATE PRONUNCIATION	EXAMPLE
b d f k l m n p q t v	pronounced as in English	
c	1 before *e* and *i* like *ch* in church	**centrale** **cinque**

Pronunciation

	2 elsewhere like *c* in cat		**casa**
ch	like *c* in cat		**che**
g	1 before *e* and *i* like *j* in jump		**gente**
			giardino
	2 elsewhere like *g* in get		**gatto**
gh	like *g* in get		**ghiaccio**
gl	like *lli* in million		**figlio**
gn	like *ni* in onion		**bagno**
h	always silent in Italian		**hanno**
r	always trilled, like the Scottish *r*		**vero**
s	1 usually like *s* in sew		**casa**
			basta
	2 sometimes like *s* in rose		**chiuso**
sc	1 before *e* and *i* like *sh* in ship		**scendere**
			scienza
	2 elsewhere like *sk* in skip		**scala**
z	1 usually like *ts* in fits		**zio**
	2 sometimes like *ds* in beads		**mezzo**

Stress

Italian words are usually stressed on the last syllable but one. When the stress falls on the last syllable this carries an accent mark, e.g. **città**, **martedì**. Sometimes the stress falls on the last syllable but two, in which case the accented syllable is not marked, as in the third person plural, present tense of verbs, e.g. **comprano**, **vendono**.

2

A Little Grammar in Action

Nouns

All nouns in Italian are either masculine or feminine whether they refer to living beings or inanimate objects. Most nouns ending in *-o* are masculine and most ending in *-a* are feminine. Those ending in *-e* may be either masculine or feminine.

Before masculine nouns the word for 'the' (or definite article) is **il**, but changes to **lo** before a word beginning with *s-* plus a consonant or *z*, and to **l'** before a word beginning with a vowel:

il libro the book
il padre the father

lo specchio the mirror
l'amico the friend

Before feminine nouns the word for 'the' is **la**, which is shortened to **l'** if the word begins with a vowel:

la donna the woman
la madre the mother

l'amica the friend
l'entrata the entrance

In the plural masculine nouns, whether ending in *-o* or *-e* in the singular, change these endings to *-i*. The word for 'the' is usually **i** but changes to **gli** before a word beginning with *s-* plus a consonant, *z* or a vowel:

i libri the books
i padri the fathers

3

gli specchi the mirrors
gli amici the friends

In the plural feminine nouns ending in *-a* change to *-e* and those ending in *-e* change to *-i*. The word for 'the' is **le**.

le donne the women
le madri the mothers

The word for 'a' is **un** before a masculine noun, but changes to **uno** before a word beginning with *s-* plus a consonant or *z*. The word for 'a' is **una** before a feminine noun but changes to **un'** before a word beginning with a vowel:

un treno a train
uno specchio a mirror

una donna a woman
un'amica a friend

Prepositions

When followed by the definite article six of the most common prepositions (**a** at, to, **di** of, **da** from, **in** in, into, **su** on, over and **con** with) are joined to it in the following pattern:

	+il	+lo	+l'	+la	+i	+gli	+le
a	al	allo	all'	alla	ai	agli	alle
da	dal	dallo	dall'	dalla	dai	dagli	dalle
di	del	dello	dell'	della	dei	degli	delle
in	nel	nello	nell'	nella	nei	negli	nelle
su	sul	sullo	sull'	sulla	sui	sugli	sulle
con	col				coi		

al negozio to the shop
nello specchio in the mirror
della donna of the woman
sulle tavole on the tables

Adjectives

The endings of adjectives depend on whether the noun they accompany is masculine, feminine or plural. Adjectives generally end in -o in the masculine and form the feminine by changing -o to -a. Those ending in -e have the same form in both masculine and feminine. Adjectives form their plural in the same way as nouns: -o changes to -i, -a to -e and -e to -i.

il libro rosso the red book
i libri rossi the red books

la piccola casa the little house
le piccole case the little houses

la porta verde the green door
le porte verdi the green doors

Note In Italian adjectives generally follow their nouns, but some, like **piccolo(a)** above, frequently precede them.

Demonstrative Adjectives

The words for 'this' and 'these' are as follows:

questo libro this book
questi libri these books
questa casa this house
queste case these houses

When **questo** or **questa** comes before a singular word beginning with a vowel it loses its final vowel:

quest' albero this tree
questi alberi these trees

The word for 'that' is **quello,** which changes in the same way as **del, dello,** listed in the section on prepositions above.

Grammar

Possessive Adjectives

The words for 'my', 'your', 'his' etc. change their form according to whether the noun they refer to is masculine, feminine or plural.

	SINGULAR		PLURAL	
	MASC	FEM	MASC	FEM
my	il mio	la mia	i miei	le mie
your	il tuo	la tua	i tuoi	le tue
his/her/its	il suo	la sua	i suoi	le sue
our	il nostro	la nostra	i nostri	le nostre
your	il vostro	la vostra	i vostri	le vostre
their	il loro	la loro	i loro	le loro

il mio libro my book
i miei libri my books

la tua valigia your suitcase
le tue valigie your suitcases

il suo cane his/her dog
i suoi cani his/her dogs

il nostro cavallo our horse
i nostri cavalli our horses

la vostra macchina your car
le vostre macchine your cars

il loro giornale their newspaper
i loro giornali their newspapers

Personal Pronouns

The words for 'I', 'you', 'he' etc. are as follows.

1 When used as the subject of a verb:

io canto	I sing
tu canti	you sing
egli canta	he sings
essa canta	she sings
Lei canta (pol. form)	you sing
noi cantiamo	we sing
voi cantate	you sing
loro cantano	they sing
Loro cantano (pol. form)	you sing

2 When used as the direct object of a verb:

Il Signor Rossi mi conosce	Mr Rossi knows me
ti	you
lo	him
la	her
La (pol. form)	you
ci	us
vi	you
li (masc.)	them
le (fem.)	them
Li (masc. pol. form)	you
Le (fem. pol. form)	you

3 When used as the indirect object of a verb:

Il Signor Rossi mi parla	Mr Rossi speaks to me
ti	you
gli	him
le	her
Le (pol. form)	you
ci	us
vi	you
Il Signor Rossi parla loro	them
Loro (pol. form)	you

Except for **loro** and **Loro**, these pronouns are always placed in front of the verb.

4 When used after a preposition:

Questi libri sono per me	These books are for me
te	you
lui	him
lei	her
Lei (pol. form)	you
noi	us
voi	you
loro	them
Loro (pol. form)	you

In Italian the polite way of addressing people is in the third person. Thus 'you' is translated by **Lei, La**, and **Le** when talking to one person and **Le** and **Loro** when talking to more than one. **Tu**, etc., and its plural **voi** are the familiar forms and should only be used when speaking to children, relatives and close friends. When written with a small 'l' **lei** means 'she' or 'her' and **loro** 'they' or 'them'.

Verbs

The whole subject of Italian verbs is too complicated for detailed discussion in a phrase book but for the traveller who wants a quick grasp of verbs with which he can communicate while staying in Italy the following basic rules will be useful.

Regular Verbs

Most Italian verbs are regular in their formation and fall into one of three categories or conjugations.

1 Verbs ending in *-are* in the infinitive.
2 Verbs ending in *-ere* in the infinitive.

comprare	to buy	credere	to believe
io compro	I buy	io credo	I believe
tu compri		tu credi	you believe
egli/essa compra	you buy he/she buys	egli/essa crede	you believe he/she believes
Lei compra	you buy	Lei crede	you believe
noi compriamo	we buy	noi crediamo	we believe
voi comprate	you buy	voi credete	you believe
loro comprano	they buy	loro credono	they believe
Loro comprano	you buy	Loro credono	you believe

Grammar

3 Verbs ending in *-ire* in the infinitive.

sentire	to hear	**finire**	to finish, end
io sento	I hear	**io finisco**	I finish
tu senti	you hear	**tu finisci**	you finish
egli/essa		**egli/essa**	
sente	he/she hears	**finisce**	he/she finishes
Lei sente	you hear	**Lei finisce**	you finish
noi sentiamo	we hear	**noi finiamo**	we finish
voi sentite	you hear	**voi finite**	you finish
loro sentono	they hear	**loro finiscono**	they finish
Loro sentono	you hear	**Loro finiscono**	you finish

To form the negative of a verb **non** is placed before it.

non compriamo libri we don't buy books

Note that the personal subject pronouns, **io, tu, noi,** etc., are usually omitted before verbs except when emphasis or clarity require their use.

Irregular Verbs

The following are a few of the more useful common irregular verbs.

essere	to be	**avere**	to have
io sono	I am	**io ho**	I have
tu sei	you are	**tu hai**	you have
egli/essa è	he/she is	**egli/essa ha**	he/she has
Lei è	you are	**Lei ha**	you have
noi siamo	we are	**noi abbiamo**	we have
voi siete	you are	**voi avete**	you have
loro sono	they are	**loro hanno**	they have
Loro sono	you are	**Loro hanno**	you have

andare	to go	**dire**	to say
io vado	I go	**io dico**	I say
tu vai	you go	**tu dici**	you say
egli/essa va	he/she goes	**egli/essa dice**	he/she says
Lei va	you go	**Lei dice**	you say
noi andiamo	we go	**noi diciamo**	we say
voi andate	you go	**voi dite**	you say
loro vanno	they go	**loro dicono**	they say
Loro vanno	you go	**Loro dicono**	you say
dovere	to have to	**fare**	to do, make
io devo	I must	**io faccio**	I do
tu devi	you must	**tu fai**	you do
egli/essa deve	he/she must	**egli/essa fa**	he/she does
Lei deve	you must	**Lei fa**	you do
noi dobbiamo	we must	**noi facciamo**	we do
voi dovete	you must	**voi fate**	you do
loro devono	they must	**loro fanno**	they do
Loro devono	you must	**Loro fanno**	you do
potere	to be able to	**sapere**	to know
io posso	I can	**io so**	I know
tu puoi	you can	**tu sai**	you know
egli/essa può	he/she can	**egli/essa sa**	he/she knows
Lei può	you can	**Lei sa**	you know
noi possiamo	we can	**noi sappiamo**	we know
voi potete	you can	**voi sapete**	you know
loro possono	they can	**loro sanno**	they know
Loro possono	you can	**Loro sanno**	you know

Grammar

venire	to come	volere	to want, wish
io vengo	I come	**io voglio**	I want
tu vieni	you come	**tu vuoi**	you want
egli/essa viene	he/she comes	**egli/essa vuole**	he/she wants
Lei viene	you come	**Lei vuole**	you want
noi veniamo	we come	**noi vogliamo**	we want
voi venite	you come	**voi volete**	you want
loro vengono	they come	**loro vogliono**	they want
Loro vengono	you come	**Loro vogliono**	you want

Italian Spoken

Italian is spoken in Italy and its islands, Sicily and Sardinia, and the offshore islands like Capri and Ischia, which are an extension of the mainland. The main differences in the Italian language are between the north and the south where there is not only a change in the way words are pronounced, but entirely different dialects. The most important cities of Italy summarize the difference in lifestyle of the regions around them.

ROME the capital is regarded by Italians as a place apart and the Romans like to think that they are superior to all other Italians. With the long history and enormous artistic treasures of Rome and the Vatican City, it is not surprising that Romans consider themselves apart. In the surrounding countryside are interesting villages and castles and good vineyards.

MILAN is the commercial capital of Italy and it lives up to its reputation. In this bustling, thriving city there are relics of the past in the Cathedral, the Church of Saint Ambrose and the Sforza Castle, and there is also the Scala Theatre. From here it is easy to reach the Italian lakes and the Alpine valleys of Piedmont.

VENICE, once a great maritime power, is still a remarkable city and packed with palaces, churches and art galleries. From Venice itself one can explore the whole lagoon with its islands: Murano where the glass is made, Burano, a fishermen's village and lacemaking centre, and Torcello with its mosaic-encrusted church echoing Ravenna.

FLORENCE, unlike Venice, which is all colour and atmosphere, is austere and formal but equally rich in art treasure. Florence is the native city of Michelangelo and other great figures of the Renaissance and the flair for design lives here still. Besides the two great art galleries, there are palaces, the famous Ponte Vecchio bridge and good vineyards all around.

NAPLES The Bay of Naples is full of echoes of the seafarers of the past from the time of Ulysses. The Romans left towns like Pompeii and Herculaneum and later invaders extended the city of Naples, which sprawls over the hills. Today it is a hectic, overpopulated metropolis but across the bay is the island of Capri and the dramatic Amalfi coast where the Neapolitans go to get away from the rush and bustle of their daily life.

THE ITALIAN ISLANDS Sardinia is still largely unspoilt and undeveloped except in a few resort areas. The people of the interior live frugal lives and use horses and donkeys for transport. The chief port in the north west is Alghero and in the south Cagliari.

SICILY was inhabited by the Greeks and the Romans and has much of historical interest as well as volcanic Mount Etna and resorts like Taormina. The towns and villages are perched on hills and the Sicilian communities are close knit; hence the success of the Mafia. Capri, Ischia and Elba, the offshore islands, are holiday resorts. They lack the individuality of the larger islands, though they offer more comforts to the visitor.

Wherever you travel in Italy you will find a few words spoken in their language will help to establish a friendly atmosphere.

Here to start with are some simple expressions of greeting and leave taking:

Good morning	**Buon giorno**
Good afternoon	**Buon giorno**
Good evening	**Buona sera**

Good night	**Buona notte**
How are you?	**Come sta?**
I'm very pleased to meet you.	**Piacere di conoscerLa**
How do you do?	**Piacere**
Goodbye	**ArrivederLa**

And some words of courtesy:

Please	**Per favore**
Thank you	**Grazie**
It's very kind of you	**Molto gentile da parte sua**
You are welcome	**Prego**
Not at all	**Di niente**

And some questions:

Where is the hotel?	**Dov'è l'albergo?**
What are you saying?	**Che cosa sta dicendo?**
When does the train leave?	**Quando parte il treno?**
Who are you?	**Chi è Lei?**
How much does it cost?	**Quanto costa?**
Which is the road to ...?	**Qual'è la strada per ...?**
Why are we waiting?	**Perché stiamo aspettando?**

Finally some useful common phrases:

Why?	**Perchè?**
How?	**Come?**
When?	**Quando?**
What?	**Che cosa?**
Where?	**Dove?**
How much?	**Quanto?**
How many?	**Quanti?**

Please speak slowly.	**Per favore parli lentamente.**
I do not understand Italian very well.	**Non capisco l'italiano molto bene.**
Will you write it down, please?	**Può scriverlo, per favore?**
How do I say ...?	**Come si dice ...?**

What is the meaning of . . . ?	**Che cosa significa . . . ?**
Please explain how this works.	**Mi può spiegare come funziona questo, per favore?**
How far is it to . . . ?	**Quanto è lontano da . . . ?**
Where is the nearest . . . ?	**Dov'è il più vicino . . . ?**
What time is it?	**Che ora è?**
Will you please help me?	**Può aiutarmi, per piacere?**
Can you point to where we are on this map?	**Può indicarmi su questa mappa dove siamo?**
Which way do I go?	**Da che parte vado?**
Is there an official tourist office here?	**C'è nessun ufficio del turismo qui vicino?**
Where is the station/bus terminus/bus stop?	**Dov'è la stazione/il capolinea degli autobus/la fermata dell'autobus?**
Where do I buy a ticket?	**Dove posso comprare il biglietto?**
Am I too early?	**Sono arrivato(a) troppo presto?**
It is too late.	**È troppo tardi.**
We have missed the train.	**Abbiamo perso il treno.**
Do I turn right/left?	**Devo girare a destra/sinistra?**
Do I go straight ahead?	**Devo andare sempre dritto?**
What is the name of this street?	**Come si chiama questa strada?**
How do I get to . . . ?	**Come arrivo a . . . ?**
How much does it cost?	**Quanto costa questo?**

It is too expensive.	**È troppo caro.**
Please give me the change.	**Mi dia il resto, per piacere.**
I am tired.	**Sono stanco(a).**
I am hungry/thirsty.	**Ho fame/ho sete.**
It is very hot/cold.	**Fa molto caldo/freddo.**
Please take me to my hotel.	**Mi porti al mio albergo, per piacere.**
Is the service included?	**Il servizio è compreso?**
Thank you very much.	**Molte grazie.**
Yes.	**Sì.**
No.	**No.**

And some idiomatic expressions:

Go away.	**Vada via.**
Leave me alone.	**Mi lasci in pace.**
Shut up.	**Chiudi la bocca.**
Oh hell!	**Al diavolo.**
How goes it?	**Come va?**
So so.	**Così e così.**
You're joking.	**Sta scherzando.**
Don't move.	**Fermo.**
That's it.	**Ecco.**
You're right.	**Ha ragione.**
Carry on.	**Vada avanti.**

All Aboard

Journeys through Italy are made easy by the excellent means of communication and interesting because of the centuries of history that have left their mark on every town and village. Air travel is, of course, the quickest way to get about and internal airlines provide an excellent service. But travel by train and coach or car is the more rewarding. Railways travel through some beautiful scenery on routes such as Milan to Rome and Cortina to Venice. The highways, too, are well cared for and the autoroutes superb, with good catering facilities as well as smooth road surfaces. Service stations are plentiful and garages helpful. Best of all are the little roads where travel is slow but every minute is a joy if you are not in a hurry. This is where you reach the heart of the country and where even a halting conversation can create a warmth of communication that remains a long time in the memory.

Arrivals and Departures

Going through Passport Control and Customs

At most of the main gateway airports and ports there will be someone with a smattering of English, but this is not the case at all frontier posts. It is useful therefore to know one or two basic phrases; apart from making communication easier, they help to establish a friendly relationship with officials and often smooth the passage through frontiers.

Good morning/afternoon/ evening.	**Buon giorno/buon giorno/ buona sera.**
I am on holiday/on business.	**Sono in vacanza/qui per affari.**
visiting relatives/friends.	**qui per vedere i miei parenti/amici.**

19

Here is my passport.	**Ecco il mio passaporto.**
Here is my vaccination certificate.	**Ecco il mio certificato di vaccinazione.**
The visa is stamped on page ...	**Il visto è a pagina ...**
They did not stamp my passport at the entry port.	**Non hanno timbrato il mio passaporto all' entrata.**
Will you please stamp my passport? It will be a souvenir of my holiday.	**Può timbrarmi il passaporto, per favore? Sarà un ricordo della mia vacanza.**
I will be staying a few days/two weeks/a month.	**Mi fermerò qualque giorno/ due settimane/un mese.**
I am just passing through.	**Sono solamente di passaggio.**
My wife and I have a joint passport.	**Mia moglie ed io abbiamo un passaporto in comune.**
The children are on my wife's passport.	**I bambini sono sul passaporto di mia moglie.**
I didn't realize it had expired.	**Non mi ero accorto che fosse scaduto.**
Can I telephone the British Consulate?	**Posso telefonare al Consolato britannico?**
I have nothing to declare.	**Non ho niente da dichiarare.**
Do you want me to open my cases? Which one?	**Devo aprire le mie valigie? Quale?**
They are all my personal belongings.	**Sono tutti oggetti personali.**
I have a few small gifts for my friends.	**Ho qualche regalo per i miei amici.**

I have 200 cigarettes, some wine and a bottle of spirits.	Ho duecento sigarette, del vino e una bottiglia di liquore.
They are for my personal consumption.	Sono per uso personale.
Do I have to pay duty?	Devo pagare il dazio?
I have no other luggage.	Non ho altri bagagli.
Do you want to see my handbag/briefcase?	Vuole vedere la mia borsetta/valigetta?
I can't find my keys.	Non riesco a trovare le chiavi.
I have 200,000 lire in currency and £100 in traveller's cheques.	Ho duecento mila lire in valuta, e cento sterline in assegni turistici.
I can't afford to pay duty.	Non ho abbastanza denaro per pagare il dazio.
Can you keep it in bond?	È possibile lasciarlo in deposito?
Here is a list of the souvenirs I have bought.	Ecco l'elenco dei souvenirs che ho comprato.
You haven't marked my suitcase.	Non ha segnato la mia valigia.
May I leave now?	Posso andare?

21

At Airports, Terminals and Stations.

Where can I find a porter?

  a luggage trolley?
  the left luggage office?
  my registered luggage?

Have you seen the representative of my travel company?

Take my bag to the bus/taxi/car.

How much per case?

Dove posso trovare un facchino?

  un carrello per i bagagli?
  il deposito bagagli?
  il mio bagaglio al seguito?

Ha visto il rappresentante della mia agenzia di viaggi?

Porti la mia borsa all'autobus/al tassì/alla macchina.

Quanto per valigia?

Toilets

Is there a ladies'/gentlemen's toilet?

Have you any soap?
  toilet paper?
  a clean towel?
  a comb or hairbrush?

Shall I leave a tip?

C'è una toilette per signore/ per uomini?

Ha del sapone?
  della carta igienica?
  un asciugamano pulito?
  un pettine o una spazzola?

Devo lasciare la mancia?

Telephone

Where are the public telephones?

I need a telephone directory.

Where can I get some change?

Dove sono i telefoni pubblici?

Vorrei un elenco del telefono.

Dove posso trovare degli spicci?

Can I dial this number or do I ask the operator?	**Posso fare questo numero direttamente o devo chiedere al centralino?**
Hullo.	**Pronto.**
May I have Rome 1234?	**Vorrei Roma uno, due, tre, quattro.**
Can I reverse the charges?	**Posso addebitare la chiamata al ricevente?**
I have been cut off.	**È caduta la linea.**
You gave me the wrong number.	**Mi ha dato un numero sbagliato.**
She's not in?	**Lei non è in casa?**
Tell her I called. My name is....	**Le dica che ho chiamato. Il mio nome è....**

Signs

Booking Office	**Ufficio prenotazioni**
Cars Check-in Desk	**Accettazione autovetture**
Coach Station	**Stazione autocorriere/ pullman**
Escalator	**Scala mobile**
Exit	**Uscita**
Information Office	**Ufficio Informazioni**
Left Luggage	**Deposito bagagli**
Platform	**Binario**
Porters	**Facchini**
Toilet	**Ritirata/W.C./Toilette/ Gabinetti**

23

Airports, Terminals and Stations

Underground	**Metropolitana**
Waiting Room	**Sala d'aspetto**

Taxi Rank

Where can I get a taxi?	**Dove posso trovare un taxi?**
Please get me a taxi.	**Per favore mi chiami un taxi.**
Take me to Via Veneto/to this address.	**Mi vuol portare a Via Veneto/a questo indirizzo.**
How much will it cost?	**Quanto costerà?**
That's too much.	**È troppo.**
Turn right/left at the next corner.	**Giri a destra/a sinistra al prossimo angolo.**
Go straight on.	**Vada dritto.**
I'll tell you when to stop.	**Le dirò io quando fermare.**
Stop.	**Si fermi.**
I'm in a hurry.	**Ho fretta.**
Take it easy.	**Vada con calma.**
Can you please carry my bags?	**Può portarmi i bagagli?**

Newsstand (Kiosk)

Have you got an English paper/magazine? any paperbacks?	**Ha un giornale/una rivista inglese?** **libri economici?**
Which is the local paper?	**Qual'è il giornale locale?**
Do you sell timetables?	**Vende orari?**

Have you a map/guide to the city?	**Ha una mappa/guida della città?**
Have you any writing paper and envelopes?	**Ha carta da lettera e buste?**
sellotape?	**nastro adesivo?**
matches?	**fiammiferi?**
stamps?	**francobolli?**
a ball-point pen?	**una penna biro?**
some string?	**dello spago?**

Information Bureau

Is there an information bureau here?	**C'è un Ufficio Informazioni qui?**
Have you any leaflets?	**Ha qualche opuscolo?**
Have you a guide to the hotels?	**Ha una guida degli alberghi?**
pensions?	**delle pensioni?**
youth hostels?	**degli ostelli?**
camp sites?	**dei camping?**
Do you find accommodation for visitors?	**Trovate una sistemazione per i visitatori?**
I want a first-class/second-class hotel.	**Vorrei un albergo di prima classe/di seconda classe.**
a pension.	**una pensione.**
a double room.	**una stanza doppia.**
just a single room.	**solamente una stanza singola.**
We'll go right away.	**Andremo subito.**
How do I get there?	**Come ci arrivo?**

At Airports

Where is the check-in desk?	**Dov'è l'accettazione bagagli?**

25

Airports, Terminals and Stations

Can I take this in the cabin?	**Posso portare questo a mano?**
Do I have to pay excess?	**Devo pagare per eccesso di peso?**
You haven't given me a luggage claim tag.	**Non mi ha dato la ricevuta del bagaglio.**
I've missed my flight. Can you give me another flight?	**Ho perso il mio volo. È possibile partire con un altro volo?**
Is there a bar on the other side of the customs barrier?	**C'è un bar dall'altra parte della dogana?**
Where is the flight indicator?	**Dov'è la tabella dei voli?**
Is there a duty free shop?	**Dov'è il negozio duty free?**
Is there another way to go up/down other than by escalator?	**C'è solo la scala mobile per salire/scendere?**
Where can I get some flight insurance?	**Dove posso fare un'assicurazione per il volo?**
Is there a wheelchair available?	**C'è una sedia a rotelle disponibile?**

At Railway Stations

Where is the ticket office?	**Dov'è lo sportello dei biglietti?**
One first-class/second class/return ticket to Rimini.	**Un biglietto prima classe/seconda classe/andata e ritorno per Rimini.**
How much is a child's fare?	**Quanto costa un biglietto per bambini?**

Can I reserve a seat/a couchette/ a sleeping berth?	**Posso riservare un posto/una cuccetta/un posto in vagone letto?**
On the express/rapide/direct/ omnibus/autorail?	**Sull'espresso/rapido/diretto/ accellerato/per trasporto vetture?**
Is there a supplement to pay?	**Devo pagare un supplemento?**
Do I have to change?	**Devo cambiare?**
Will there be a restaurant car/ buffet car on the train?	**C'è un vagone ristorante/un buffet sul treno?**
Where is the platform for the train to Naples?	**Dov'è il binario del treno per Napoli?**
Does my friend need a platform ticket?	**Il mio amico ha bisogno di un biglietto per accompagnarmi al treno?**
At what time does the train leave?	**A che ora parte il treno?**

At a Port

Which is quay number six?	**Qual'è la banchina numero sei?**
Where is the car ferry terminal?	**Da dove parte il traghetto per le macchine?**
At what time can I go on board?	**A che ora posso essere a bordo?**
Will there be an announcement when visitors must disembark?	**Sarà annunciato quando i visitatori dovranno sbarcare?**

Airports, Terminals and Stations

VOCABULARY

porter	**il facchino**
station master	**il capostazione**
bus driver	**l'autista**
ticket collector	**il controllore**
guard	**il capotreno**
security officer	**l'ufficiale di Sicurezza**
vending machine	**il distributore automatico**
left luggage office	**il deposito bagagli**
waiting room	**la sala d'aspetto**
station buffet	**il buffet della stazione**
clock	**l'orologio**
bench	**la panchina**
gate	**il cancello**
tannoy	**l'alto parlante**
locker	**la cassetta di sicurezza**

En Route

General Expressions

At what time do we start/take off?	A che ora si parte/si decolla?
Why is there a delay?	Perchè c'è un ritardo?
Have I got time to go to the toilet?	Ho il tempo di andare alla toilette?
I have mislaid my ticket.	Ho perduto il mio biglietto.
Take my address and passport number.	Prenda nota del mio indirizzo e del numero del mio passaporto.
Is this seat reserved?	Questo posto è prenotato?

Travelling by Air

Are you the Chief Steward/Stewardess?	È Lei lo Steward/l'Hostess?
Which button do I press to call you?	Quale bottone devo premere per chiamarLa?
Can you help me to adjust my seat?	Mi può aiutare a sistemare il sedile?
I haven't got a sick bag.	Non ho una busta di carta, in caso mi senta male.
How high are we flying?	A che altezza voliamo?
What speed are we doing?	A che velocità andiamo?

Travelling

What town is that down there?	**Come si chiama la città laggiù?**
Is there a map of the route?	**Ha una mappa della rotta?**
Are there any duty-free goods available?	**È possibile comprare qualcosa esente dal dazio?**
Can I pay you in foreign currency/English money?	**È possibile pagare in valuta straniera/con valuta inglese?**
The airvent is stuck.	**Il ventilatore non funziona.**
May I change my seat?	**Posso cambiare posto?**

VOCABULARY

aircraft	**l'apparecchio**
ashtray	**il posacenere**
flight deck	**la cabina di pilotaggio**
fuselage	**la fusoliera**
jet engine	**il motore a reazione**
light	**la luce**
air terminal	**l'air terminal**
luggage shelf	**il portabagagli**
propeller	**l'elica**
tail	**la coda**
tray meal	**il vassoio**
window	**il finestrino**
wing	**l'ala**
arrival gate	**il cancello d'arrivo**

SIGNS

Fasten your seat belt	**Allacciare le cinture**
Emergency Exit	**Uscita d'emergenza**
No Smoking	**Vietato fumare**

30

Travelling by Motor Rail

I have booked my car by motor rail to Turin.	**Ho prenotato un posto sul treno per Torino per la mia macchina.**
Does the ticket include insurance?	**È inclusa l'assicurazione nel biglietto?**
At what time must I report?	**A che ora mi devo presentare?**
Where is the loading platform?	**Da dove si fa salire la macchina?**
Shall I lock the car?	**Devo chiudere la macchina?**
Can I leave my belongings in the car?	**Posso lasciare la mia roba in macchina?**
Where is our compartment?	**Dov'è il nostro scompartimento?**
At what time do I have to drive off?	**A che ora devo portare fuori la macchina?**

Travelling by Rail

Can you tell me where carriage 5 is?	**Mi può dire dov'è il vagone numero cinque?**
I have a couchette reservation.	**Ho la prenotazione per la cuccetta.**
This is my seat reservation.	**Ecco la prenotazione del mio posto.**
Is this seat taken?	**Questo posto è occupato?**
Is the dining car at the front or back?	**Il vagone ristorante è davanti o dietro?**

Travelling

Two tickets for the first service, please.	**Due biglietti per il primo turno, per favore.**
Is the buffet car open throughout the journey?	**Il buffet è aperto durante il viaggio?**
Can I leave my big case in the baggage car?	**Posso lasciare questa grande valigia nel vagone-bagagli?**
Is there an observation car?	**C'è un vagone panoramico?**
What station is this?	**Che stazione è questa?**
The heating is on/off/too high/too low.	**Il riscaldamento è acceso/è spento/ è troppo alto/è troppo basso.**
I can't open/close the window.	**Non riesco ad aprire/ chiudere il finestrino.**
Where do I have to change?	**Dove devo cambiare?**
Is this where I get my connection for Milan?	**È qui che devo prendere la coincidenza per Milano?**

VOCABULARY

blanket	**la coperta**
corridor	**il corridoio**
compartment	**lo scompartimento**
cushion	**il cuscino**
luggage rack	**il portabagagli**
non smoking	**non fumatori**
sleeping berth	**la cuccetta**
sleeping car	**il vagone letto**
sliding door	**la porta scorrevole**

SIGNS

Do not lean out of the windows	**Vietato sporgersi dai finestrini**
Do not use the toilet while the train is stationary	**Non usare la ritirata durante le fermate**

Travelling on a Steamer

Where is the purser's office?	**Dov'è l'Ufficio dell'Ufficiale commissario?**
Can you show me my cabin?	**Può mostrarmi la cabina?**
Are you the steward?	**È Lei lo steward?**
Is there a children's nursery/a shop/a gymnasium?	**C'è un asilo per i bambini/un negozio/una palestra?**
Where can I get seasick tablets?	**Dove posso trovare delle pillole contro il mal di mare?**
On which side do we disembark?	**Da quale parte si sbarca?**
The sea is calm/rough.	**Il mare è calmo/agitato.**
What are those birds – seagulls?	**Che uccelli sono – gabbiani?**
Is there a duty-free shop?	**C'è un negozio duty free?**

VOCABULARY

aft	**la poppa**
anchor	**l'ancora**
bridge	**il ponte di comando**
captain	**il capitano**
crew	**l'equipaggio**

33

Travelling

deck	**il ponte**
funnel	**il fumaiolo**
lifebelt	**il salvagente**
officer	**l'Ufficiale**
lifeboat	**la barca di salvataggio**
mast	**l'albero**
port (left)	**il babordo**
propeller	**il propulsore**
radar	**il radar**
raft	**la zattera di salvataggio**
rail	**il parapetto**
starboard (right)	**il tribordo**

Travelling by Coach

Is this the coach for Bologna?	**È questa la corriera per Bologna?**
Can I sit near the driver?	**Posso sedermi vicino al conducente?**
Are the seats numbered?	**I sedili sono numerati?**
Do I pay on the coach?	**Devo pagare sulla corriera?**
Is there a stop en route?	**C'è una fermata su questo tragitto?**
Would you mind closing the window? It's draughty.	**Le dispiace chiudere il finestrino? C'è corrente.**
Can you help me with my luggage?	**Mi può aiutare a sistemare il bagaglio?**

VOCABULARY

back seat	**il sedile posteriore**
driver	**il conducente/l'autista**

34

foot rest	**il poggiapiedi**
front seat	**il sedile anteriore**
guide	**la guida**
luggage compartment	**il portabagagli**

Buses and Metro

Where is the bus stop?	**Dov'è la fermata dell'autobus?**
Does one have to queue?	**Si deve fare la fila?**
Can I buy a book of tickets?	**Posso fare un abbonamento?**
Do you go by the Forum?	**Va dalle parti del Foro?**
Will you tell me when we reach the Piazza di Spagna?	**Può avvertirmi quando siamo a Piazza di Spagna?**
I want to get off at the next stop.	**Voglio scendere alla prossima fermata.**
Will you ring the bell please?	**Può suonare il campanello, per favore?**
I want to go to the Borghese Gardens.	**Vorrei andare a Villa Borghese.**
Which line do I take?	**Quale linea devo prendere?**
Do I have to change?	**Devo cambiare?**
At what time is the last metro?	**A che ora è l'ultima metropolitana?**

<small>VOCABULARY</small>

automatic door	**la porta automatica**
barrier	**la barriera**
escalator	**la scala mobile**

Travelling

Reserved for the disabled

Riservato agli invalidi

Other Vehicles

Where can I hire a bicycle/
tandem?

**Dove posso affittare una
bicicletta/un tandem?**

Please put some air in this tyre.

**Può gonfiare questa ruota,
per favore?**

One of the spokes is broken.

Uno dei raggi è rotto.

The brake is not working.

Il freno non funziona.

Do you have a bicycle with
gears?

**Ha una bicicletta con il
cambio?**

The saddle needs lowering/
raising.

**Bisogna abbassare/alzare il
sellino.**

Are there any horse-drawn
vehicles at this resort?

**Ci sono cavalli, veicoli da
traino in questo posto?**

Will you put the roof down
please?

**Può abbassare il tetto per
favore?**

Will you take the children on the
driver's box?

**È possibile tenere i bambini
vicino al conducente?**

Is the cable car working?

La funivia è in funzione?

Is there a chair lift?

C'è una seggiovia?

Please adjust the safety bar for
me.

**Può sistemare la sbarra di
sicurezza?**

Do they run frequently?

Passano di frequente?

How high is the upper station?

**A che altezza è la stazione
più alta?**

Can I walk down?	**Posso andare giù a piedi?**
Is it possible to get a weekly/monthly ticket?	**È possibile fare una tessera settimanale/mensile?**

VOCABULARY

bicycle pump	**la pompa di bicicletta**
carrier	**il portabagagli**
chain	**la catena**
crossbar	**la canna (della bicicletta)**
donkey	**l'asino**
handlebars	**il manubrio**
harness	**i finimenti**
lamp	**il fanale**
mudguard	**il parafango**
pedal	**il pedale**
rear lights	**le luci posteriori**
ski-lift	**lo skilift**
skis	**gli sci**
sledge	**la slitta**
toboggan	**il toboga**
whip	**la cinghia**

Walking About

IN TOWN

Is this the main shopping street?	**È questa la via principale per fare spese?**
Where is the town hall/police station?	**Dov'è il Municipio/la questura?**
Can you direct me to the Tourist Office?	**Può indicarmi l'Ufficio del Turismo?**

37

Travelling

In what part of town are the theatres/nightclubs?	**In quale parte della città sono i teatri/i nightclubs?**
Can I get there by bus/underground/on foot?	**Posso arrivarci in autobus/in metropolitana/a piedi?**
Where is the nearest station/stop?	**Dov'è la stazione/la fermata più vicina?**
Is there a market in the town?	**C'è un mercato in questa città?**
What day is market day?	**Qual'è il giorno di mercato?**
Is the business centre near?	**Il centro degli affari è vicino?**
Must one cross at the traffic lights?	**Si deve attraversare al semaforo?**
Do pedestrians have right of way here?	**I pedoni hanno diritto di precedenza qui?**
Is there a public toilet near?	**Ci sono gabinetti pubblici qui vicino?**

VOCABULARY

castle	**il castello**
cathedral	**la cattedrale**
cemetery	**il cimitero**
church	**la chiesa**
city centre	**il centro**
concert hall	**la sala dei concerti**
courtyard	**il cortile**
docks	**la banchina**
exhibition	**la mostra**
factory	**la fabbrica**
fortress	**la fortezza**
fountain	**la fontana**
government buildings	**i palazzi pubblici**

gardens	**i giardini**
harbour	**il porto**
lake	**il lago**
monastery	**il monastero**
monument	**il monumento**
museum	**il museo**
old town	**la città vecchia**
opera house	**il teatro dell'opera**
palace	**il palazzo**
park	**il parco**
ruins	**le rovine**
shopping centre	**i negozi**
stadium	**lo stadio**
statue	**la statua**
stock exchange	**la borsa**
subway	**il sottopassaggio**
traffic lights	**il semaforo**
tower	**la torre**
university	**l'università**
zoo	**lo zoo**

IN THE COUNTRY

May we walk through here?	**Possiamo passare da qui?**
Is this a public footpath?	**Questo è un sentiero pubblico?**
Do I need permission to fish?	**Ho bisogno di una licenza di pesca?**
Which way is north/south/east/ west?	**Da che parte è il nord/sud/ l'est/ovest?**
Is there a bridge or ford across this stream?	**C'è un ponte o un guado per attraversare questo torrente?**
How far is the nearest village?	**Quanto dista il più vicino villaggio?**

39

Travelling

I am lost. Can you please direct me to ...?	**Mi sono perso. Può dirigermi verso ...?**
Will you please show me the route on this map?	**Può mostrarmi la strada su questa mappa, per piacere?**

Vocabulary

barn	**il granaio**
bird	**l'uccello**
brook	**il ruscello**
canal	**il canale**
cliff	**il precipizio**
cottage	**il cottage**
cow	**la mucca**
dog	**il cane**
farm	**la fattoria**
field	**il campo**
footpath	**il sentiero**
forest	**la foresta**
goat	**la capra**
heath	**la brughiera**
hill	**la collina**
horse	**il cavallo**
inn	**l'osteria**
lake	**il lago**
marsh	**la palude**
moorland	**la landa**
mountain	**la montagna**
orchard	**il frutteto**
peak	**la cima**
pond	**lo stagno**
river	**il fiume**
sea	**il mare**
sheep	**la pecora**
spring	**la sorgente**

40

stream	il torrente
swamp	il pantano
tree	l'albero
valley	la valle
village	il villaggio
vineyard	la vigna
waterfall	la cascata
well	il pozzo
wood	il bosco

Motoring

At the Frontier

Here is my registration book/green card insurance/driving licence.	**Ecco il mio libretto di circolazione/la carta verde/la patente.**
I have an international licence.	**Ho una patente internazionale.**
This is a translation of my British licence.	**Ecco la traduzione della mia patente britannica.**
This is a self-drive car. Here are the documents.	**Questa è una macchina in affitto. Ecco i documenti.**
Do you want to open the boot?	**Vuole aprire il portabagagli?**
I arrived today.	**Sono arrivato oggi.**
I am staying for two weeks.	**Mi fermerò due settimane.**
Does this customs post close at night?	**La Frontiera è chiusa di notte?**
At what time does it close?	**A che ora chiude?**
Do you sell petrol coupons?	**Vendete coupons per la benzina?**
Shall I leave my engine running?	**Devo lasciare il motore acceso?**
Do you want me to stop the engine?	**Devo spegnere il motore?**

On the Road

Italian roads are classified as follows:–

Autostrada	**A**
Strada Nazionale	**SS**
Strada Provinciale	**D**

Autoroutes are excellent but you have to pay to drive on them, which can be quite expensive. On the autoroutes there are good service areas and excellent restaurants which are licensed. National and provincial roads go through towns and villages which you would miss on the autoroute. Country roads are narrow and picturesque – perfect if you are not in a hurry and want to absorb the atmosphere of the region through which you are travelling.

Can you tell me how to get to Pisa?	**Mi può dire come si arriva a Pisa?**
How many kilometres is it?	**Quanti chilometri dista?**
Is it a good road?	**È una buona strada?**
Is it hilly/flat/straight/winding?	**È ondulata/piana/dritta/a curve?**
What is the speed limit on this section?	**Qual'è il limite di velocità in questo punto?**
Will you point out the route on this map please?	**Mi può indicare la strada su questa cartina, per favore?**
How much does this section of motorway cost?	**Quanto costa questa parte di autostrada?**
Do I pay at the exit?	**Devo pagare all'uscita?**
I am sorry I have no change.	**Mi dispiace non ho spicci.**

Motoring

How far is it to the next petrol station?	**Quanto è lontana la prossima stazione di servizio?**
I want twenty five litres, please.	**Vorrei venticinque litri, per favore.**
Give me 10,000 lire worth.	**Mi dia benzina per dieci mila lire.**
Fill her up.	**Faccia il pieno.**
Please check the oil and water.	**Controlli l'olio e l'acqua, per favore.**
I need some air in the tyres.	**Devo gonfiare le gomme.**
I think the windscreen fluid needs topping up.	**Penso di dovere riempire il serbatoio dell'acqua per il finestrino.**
Have you any distilled water for the battery?	**Ha dell'acqua distillata per la batteria?**
Please clean the windscreen.	**Mi pulisca il finestrino, per favore.**
Have you any paper towels?	**Ha degli asciugamani di carta?**
Have you got a carwash?	**È possibile far lavare la macchina?**
Do you sell yellow filters for the headlights?	**Vendete filtri gialli per i fari?**
Can I park here?	**Posso parcheggiare qui?**
Where is the nearest car park?	**Dov'è il posteggio più vicino?**

44

Trouble with the Police

Usually the police are polite and helpful to visitors, but they
are more likely to be so if you appear friendly and
co-operative. A few phrases in their language can sometimes
work miracles.

I'm sorry, I did not see you signal.	**Mi dispiace, non ho visto il Suo segnale.**
I thought I had right of way.	**Pensavo di avere diritto di precedenza.**
I apologise. I won't do it again.	**Mi scusi, non lo farò più.**
Here is my name and address.	**Ecco il mio nome e indirizzo.**
This is my passport.	**Ecco il mio passaporto.**
Do I have to pay a fine?	**Devo pagare una multa?**
How much?	**Quanto?**
I haven't got any cash on me. Can I settle up at a police station?	**Non ho soldi con me. È possibile definire la questione alla stazione di Polizia?**
Thank you for your courtesy.	**Grazie per la sua cortesia.**

Car Rental

I want to hire a car.	**Vorrei affittare una macchina.**
a small car.	**una macchina piccola.**
a family saloon.	**una macchina familiare.**
a large car.	**una macchina grande.**
a sports car.	**una macchina sportiva.**
a van.	**un pulmino.**
I shall need it for ... days.	**Ne ho bisogno per ... giorni.**

45

Motoring

How much is the daily charge?	**Quanto costa al giorno?**
Is it cheaper by the week?	**È più economica per una settimana intera?**
Does that include mileage and insurance?	**Chilometraggio e assicurazione inclusi?**
What is the mileage charge?	**Quanto è il costo a chilometro?**
Is the insurance for car and passengers?	**L'assicurazione include la macchina e i passeggeri?**
Where do I pick up the car?	**Dove devo ritirare la macchina?**
Can you bring it to my hotel?	**La può portare al mio albergo?**
Can I leave it at another town or at the airport?	**La posso lasciare in un'altra città o all'aeroporto?**
Is there a deposit to pay?	**Devo pagare un deposito?**
May I pay with my credit card?	**Posso pagare con la mia carta di credito?**
Will you please check the documents with me?	**Può controllare i documenti insieme a me?**
Will you show me the gears and instrument panel?	**Mi può mostrare come funziona il cambio e il cruscotto?**
Is the tank full of petrol?	**C'è il pieno nel serbatoio?**

Road Signs

Autostrada	Motorway
Alt	Halt
Caduta di massi	Falling stones
Discesa pericolosa	Dangerous descent

46

Dogana	Customs
Entrata	Entrance
Incrocio	Crossroads
Incrocio pericoloso	Dangerous crossroads
Lavori in corso	Roadworks
Rallentare	Slow
Senso unico	One way
Sosta vietata	No parking
Sosta autorizzata	Parking permitted
Svolta	Curve
Uscita	Exit
Vietato l'ingresso	No entry

Trouble on the Road

OTHER PEOPLE'S

There has been an accident three miles back.	**C'è stato un incidente cinque chilometri indietro.**
Will you phone the police please?	**Può telefonare alla Polizia, per piacere?**
No, I did not see it happen.	**No, non l'ho visto accadere.**
The car registration number was....	**La targa della macchina era ...**
I do not think anyone is hurt.	**Penso che non ci siano feriti.**
Someone is badly hurt.	**Qualcuno è gravemente ferito.**

YOURS

Are you all right?	**Sta bene?**
My passengers are not hurt.	**I miei passeggeri non sono feriti.**

Motoring

The car is damaged.	**La macchina è danneggiata.**
May I have your insurance details?	**Può darmi i dettagli della Sua assicurazione?**
Your name and address please?	**Il Suo nome e indirizzo per favore?**
Will you please fill out this form?	**Può compilare questo modulo, per favore?**
I think we shall have to call the police.	**Penso che dovremmo chiamare la Polizia.**
Excuse me, would you mind being a witness?	**Scusi, Le dispiacerebbe fare da testimone?**
It happened because he put his brakes on suddenly.	**È accaduto perchè lui ha frenato all'improvviso.**
He came out of a side road without signalling.	**È uscito da una strada laterale senza segnalare.**
He tried to overtake on a narrow stretch of road.	**Ha cercato di sorpassare in una strettoia.**
He turned off without signalling.	**Ha girato senza segnalare.**
May I explain to someone who understands English?	**Potrei spiegarlo a qualcuno che capisce l'inglese?**

If you are unfortunate enough to have an accident, be sure to get all the details from the other driver involved. Your insurance company will have provided you with an accident report form. Fill it up on the spot and include the required details from the other driver. Above all, keep cool.

Breakdown

If you have a breakdown put the red triangle behind your car at once or you may be penalized. Get the car off the road if possible.

48

Thank you for stopping. I am in trouble. Will you help me?	**Grazie per essersi fermato. Sono nei pasticci. Può aiutarmi?**
My car has broken down.	**La mia macchina si è rotta.**
Will you tell the next garage or breakdown service vehicle that you pass?	**Può avvertire il prossimo garage o qualsiasi macchina dell'ACI che le capiti d'incontrare?**
Will you please telephone a garage for me?	**Può telefonare a un garage da parte mia?**
Can you give me a lift to the next telephone?	**Mi può dare un passaggio fino al prossimo telefono?**
Can you send a breakdown truck?	**Può mandarmi un carroattrezzi?**
I am five kilometres from the last entry on the motorway.	**Sono a cinque chilometri dall'ultima entrata della autostrada.**
I am three kilometres from Siena on the National Highway.	**Sono a tre chilometri da Siena sulla Strada Nazionale.**
How long will you be?	**Fra quanto tempo arriverete?**

Repairs

There's something wrong with the engine.	**C'è qualche cosa che non va nel motore.**
The clutch is slipping.	**La frizione slitta.**
There is a noise from the . . .	**C'è un rumore nel . . .**
The brakes are not working.	**I freni non funzionano.**
The water system is leaking.	**Il serbatoio dell'acqua perde.**

My fan belt is broken.	**La cinghia del ventilatore è rotta.**
I've got a flat tyre.	**Ho una gomma sgonfia.**
The electrical system has failed.	**Il circuito elettrico non funziona.**
The engine is overheating.	**Il motore è surriscaldato.**
The car won't start.	**La macchina non si mette in moto.**
What is the matter?	**Qual'è il problema?**
Is it broken?	**È rotto?**
burnt out?	**bruciato?**
disconnected?	**staccato?**
jammed?	**bloccato?**
leaking?	**Perde?**
short circuiting?	**C'è un cortocircuito?**
Do I need a new part?	**Ho bisogno di un pezzo nuovo?**
Is there a Ford agent in town?	**C'è un commissionario della Ford in città?**
Can you send for the part?	**Può mandare a prendere il pezzo?**
Is it serious?	**È grave?**
How long will it take to repair?	**Quanto tempo ci vorrá per la riparazione?**
Can I hire another car?	**Posso prendere in affitto un' altra macchina?**
What will it cost?	**Quanto costerà?**
I will get the part flown from Britain.	**Mi farò mandare il pezzo via aerea dall'Inghilterra.**

Your mechanic has been very kind. I would like to tip him.

Il suo meccanico è stato molto gentile. Vorrei lasciargli una mancia.

VOCABULARY

battery	**la batteria**
brakes	**i freni**
brake lining	**le guarnizioni dei freni**
bulbs	**le lampade**
carburettor	**il carburatore**
clutch	**la frizione**
cooling system	**il sistema di raffreddamento**
dip switch	**l'interruttore degli abbaglianti**
dynamo	**la dinamo**
distributor	**il distributore**
electrical system	**il circuito elettrico**
engine	**il motore**
exhaust pipe	**il tubo di scappamento**
fan	**il ventilatore**
filter	**il filtro**
fuel pump	**la pompa della benzina**
fuel tank	**il serbatoio della benzina**
gears	**le marce**
generator	**il generatore**
hand brake	**il freno a mano**
headlights	**i fari abbaglianti**
heating system	**il riscaldamento**
horn	**il clacson**
ignition	**l'accensione**
indicator	**la freccia**
lubrication system	**il sistema di lubrificazione**
radiator	**il radiatore**
reflectors	**i deflettori**
seat	**il sedile**
silencer	**il silenziatore**

Motoring

sparking plug	**la candela**
speedometer	**il tachimetro**
suspension	**le sospensioni**
transmission	**la trasmissione**
wheels	**le ruote**
windscreen wiper	**il tergicristallo**

A Place to Stay

There are places to stay to suit every budget level in Italy from the great luxury palaces of the Riviera to the **osteria** with rooms to let. If you have not booked a hotel in advance, ask at the Azienda Autonoma di Soggiorno of each town; they will help you find a place within your price range. If you don't want to stay at a hotel there are villas and country cottages, camping sites and rooms in private houses. The standards of comfort vary considerably, but prices are fixed by law.

Hotels and Pensions

Finding a Room

I am travelling with the . . . travel agency.	Io viaggio con l'Agenzia . . .
Here is my hotel coupon.	Ecco la ricevuta del mio albergo.
My room is already reserved.	La mia camera è già prenotata.
I am travelling independently.	Io viaggio da solo.
Will a porter bring my luggage in?	Può il facchino portare dentro il mio bagaglio?
Can I leave my car here?	Posso lasciare lì la mia macchina?
Is there a car park?	C'è un posteggio?
Are you the receptionist/concierge/manager?	Lei è la receptionist/il portiere/il direttore?

Accommodation

Have you a single room/double room/three-bedded room?
with a full size bath and separate toilet?
with bath or shower?
with a balcony?
looking over the front/the back?

Ha una camera singola/ doppia/con tre letti?
con un bagno completo e una toilette separata?
con bagno o doccia?
con balcone?
che guardi sul davanti/sul dietro?

How much is it per day?

Quanto costa al giorno?

Is there a reduction for a longer stay/for children?

C'è una riduzione per lunghi soggiorni/per bambini?

Are there special mealtimes for children?

Servite il pranzo ai bambini a un'ora particolare?

I don't want to pay more than ... lire per day.

Non voglio spendere più di ... lire al giorno.

Have you anything cheaper?

Ha niente di più economico?

Do I have to fill in a visitor's card?

Devo compilare qualche modulo?

Here is my passport.

Ecco il mio passaporto.

How long will you keep it?

Per quanto tempo lo terrete?

I'd like to go up to my room right away.

Vorrei andare subito nella mia stanza.

Will you send up the luggage?

Può mandare sù il bagaglio?

This case is for Room 3 and that one for Number 12.

Questa valigia va nella camera numero tre e questa nella numero dodici.

May I have the room key?

Posso avere la chiave della camera?

Is the key in the door?

La chiave è nella porta?

Where is the lift? Do I work it myself?	**Dov'è l'ascensore? Devo farlo funzionare da solo?**
Is breakfast included?	**La prima colazione è compresa?**
Do you do demi pension?	**Fate la mezza pensione?**
Can I put all extras on my bill?	**Posso mettere in conto tutti gli extra?**
Is there a post box in the hotel?	**C'è una cassetta delle lettere nell'albergo?**
Can you get the daily papers for me?	**È possibile avere i giornali del mattino?**

Moving In

This room is too small/large/ noisy/dark/high up.	**Questa camera è troppo piccola/grande/rumorosa/ buia/in alto.**
You haven't got a double bed?	**Non avete un letto doppio?**
Please make the twin beds into one double.	**Può unire i due letti, per favore?**
I need a child's cot.	**Posso avere un lettino per bambini?**

I shall need another pillow/ blanket.
    clothes hangers.
    some writing paper.
	**Ho bisogno di un altro cuscino/di un'altra coperta.
	    di attaccapanni.
	    di carta da lettere.**

The bedside light is not working. The bulb is broken.	**La luce vicino al letto non funziona. È rotta la lampadina.**
Which is the hot tap/the cold?	**Qual'è il rubinetto dell'acqua calda/fredda?**

Accommodation

Is this the electric razor socket?	È questa la presa per il rasoio?
What is the voltage?	Qual'è il voltaggio?
My plug won't fit. Have you an adaptor?	La mia spina non entra. Ha un riduttore?
Is there an electrician in the village?	C'è un elettricista nel paese?
Is there a hotel laundry?	C'è una lavanderia nell'albergo?
Are there facilities for washing and ironing clothes?	È possibile lavare e stirare i vestiti?
The blind is stuck.	La veneziana è bloccata.
Will you bring a bottle of drinking water?	Può portarmi una bottiglia d'acqua da bere?
Can I leave valuables in the hotel safe?	Posso lasciare i miei oggetti di valore nella cassaforte dell'albergo?
What time is breakfast/lunch/dinner?	A che ora è la colazione/il pranzo/la cena?
Do you serve breakfast in bed?	Servite la colazione in camera?
Does the hotel do packed lunches?	L'albergo prepara cestini per il pranzo?

Small Hotels and Pensions

Do you have set times for meals?	Avete orari stabiliti per i pasti?
May I have a towel and soap?	Potrei avere un asciugamano e del sapone?

56

At what time do you lock the front door at night?	A che ora chiudete il portone di notte?
May I have a key?	Posso avere una chiave?
Is it all right to leave the car in the street?	Posso lasciare la macchina in strada?
Will our things be safe?	La nostra roba sarà al sicuro?
Where is the nearest garage?	Dov'è il garage più vicino?

Rooms in Private Houses

Do you have a room free?	Ha una camera libera?
Do you do breakfast?	È possibile avere la prima colazione?
Is there a café nearby?	C'è un caffè qui vicino?
Would you like me to pay now?	Devo pagare adesso?
At what time will it be convenient to use the bathroom?	A che ora è meglio usare il bagno?
Do I need to tell you if I have a bath?	Devo avvertire se faccio un bagno?
Could you wake us in the morning?	Può svegliarci la mattina?
Is there a lounge?	C'è una sala comune?
Shall I lock my room?	Devo chiudere a chiave la mia camera?

Paying the Bill

| May I have my bill, please? | Posso avere il mio conto, per favore? |

57

Accommodation

Will you prepare my bill for first thing tomorrow?	**Può preparare il mio conto per prima cosa domani mattina?**
I think there is a mistake.	**Credo che ci sia un errore.**
I don't understand this item.	**Non capisco questo.**
May I pay by cheque?	**Posso pagare con un assegno?**
I have a Eurocheque card.	**Ho una Eurocheque card.**
Do you accept credit cards?	**Accetta carte di credito?**
Is service included?	**Il servizio è incluso?**
Is VAT included?	**L'IVA è inclusa?**
May I have a receipt please?	**Potrei avere una ricevuta?**
Please forward my mail to ...	**Per favore, inoltri la mia posta a ...**
We have enjoyed ourselves very much.	**Ci siamo divertiti molto.**
May I have one of your leaflets?	**Posso avere uno dei suoi opuscoli?**

Vocabulary

bar	**il bar**
barman	**il barista**
bed	**il letto**
chair	**la sedia**
chambermaid	**la cameriera**
children's playground	**il campo di giochi**
discothèque	**la discoteca**
door	**la porta**
hall	**l'ingresso**

lift	**l'ascensore**
light switch	**l'interruttore della luce**
lounge	**il salotto**
luggage porter	**il facchino**
manager	**il direttore**
mirror	**lo specchio**
night club	**il night**
playground	**il campo da gioco**
playroom	**la sala da gioco**
radio	**la radio**
restaurant	**il ristorante**
stairs	**le scale**
swimming pool	**la piscina**
telephone operator	**il centralino**
waiter	**il cameriere**
waitress	**la cameriera**
wardrobe	**l'armadio**
window	**la finestra**

Catering for Yourself
Villas and Apartments

I have booked a villa/apartment.	**Ho prenotato una villa/un appartamento.**
Will you please show me round it?	**Me la/lo può mostrare?**
Here is my voucher.	**Ecco la prenotazione.**
Where is the light switch/power point/fuse box?	**Dov'è l'interruttore della luce/le prese di corrente/la scatola dei fusibili?**
Do all the outside doors lock?	**Tutte le porte esterne si chiudono a chiave?**
How do the shutters work?	**Come funzionano le imposte?**
How does the hot water system work?	**Come funziona l'acqua calda?**
Where is the mains valve?	**Dov'è l'interruttore principale?**
Is there mains gas?	**C'è il gas?**
Are gas cylinders delivered?	**Portano a casa le bombole del gas?**
At what time does the house help come?	**A che ora viene la domestica?**
Can we have three sets of house keys?	**È possibile avere tre copie delle chiavi di casa?**
When is the rubbish collected?	**Quando portano via la spazzatura?**
Are the shops nearby?	**I negozi sono vicini?**

Where is the bus stop/station?	**Dov'è la fermata dell'autobus/la stazione?**
Have you a map of the area?	**Ha una mappa della zona?**

Camping

Have you a site free?	**Avete un posto libero?**
Do you rent bungalows? tents? cooking equipment?	**Affittate bungalows? tende? equipaggiamento per cucinare?**
Are there toilets? washing facilities? cooking facilities?	**Ci sono toilettes? Ci si può lavare? Ci si può cucinare?**
How much does it cost per night?	**Quanto costa a notte?**
Can I put my tent here?	**Posso mettere la mia tenda qui?**
Is there room for a trailer?	**C'è posto per un rimorchio?**
Is there a night guard?	**C'è una guardia notturna?**
Where is the camp shop? restaurant? the nearest shopping centre?	**Dov'è il negozio del campeggio? il ristorante? Dove sono i negozi più vicini?**
At what time do I have to vacate the site?	**A che ora devo lasciare libero il posto?**
Where is the drinking tap?	**Dov'è il rubinetto dell'acqua da bere?**

61

Catering for Yourself

VOCABULARY

barbecue	il barbecue
basin	il lavandino
bucket	il secchio
camping gas	il camping gas
frame tent	l'intelaiatura della tenda
grill	la griglia
guy ropes	le corde
ice-bucket	il secchiello del ghiaccio
insecticide	l'insetticida
knife	il coltello
mosquito repellant	l'insetticida
sleeping bag	il sacco a pelo
spade	la pala
tent	la tenda
tent pegs	i paletti
waterproof sheet	il telo impermeabile
stove	il fornello

Youth Hostelling

Is there a youth hostel in this town?	C'è un ostello della gioventù in questa città?
Have you room for tonight?	Avete posto per stanotte?
We are members of the Youth Hostels Association.	Siamo membri della Youth Hostels Association.
What are the house rules?	Quali sono le regole del luogo?
How long can we stay?	Quanto tempo possiamo fermarci?
Is there a youth hostel at ...?	C'è un ostello a ...?

Eating and Drinking

Meal times not only offer a chance to satisfy the appetite, but provide an intimate glimpse of the life of the places you are visiting. There are the regional specialities to savour, which reveal something of the character of the local environment. The dishes of Milan or Venice, for example, are different from those of Naples. In the former, the farms of Lombardy and the Po valley contribute good meat and fruit and vegetables. In Naples olive oil and the aromatic herbs of the warm south enrich the dishes of Mediterranean fish.

Above all, meal times provide an opportunity to watch the fascinating drama of people: the farmers at the village **osteria**, the families at Sunday lunch, the fishermen at the quayside café. Different types of restaurant satisfy different tastes and Italy offers a wide variety.

An **osteria** is an inn, a **trattoria** a typical restaurant. Cafés serve beer and coffee with a snack service. Restaurants are of various categories from one-man shows to sophisticated four-star establishments. Restaurants that specialize in grills are often called **rosticceria**. For those who travel by car, there are excellent motorway restaurants at service areas.

Can you recommend a good restaurant?	**Può raccomandarmi un buon ristorante?**
one that is not too expensive?	**uno non troppo caro?**
a typical restaurant of the region?	**un ristorante tipico della zona?**
one with music?	**uno con musica?**
a four-star establishment?	**un locale con quattro stelle?**
a Chinese/French/Neapolitan/Bolognese/Venetian restaurant?	**un ristorante cinese/francese/napoletano/bolognese/veneziano?**

Is there a good snack bar nearby?	**C'è un buono snack bar qui vicino?**
Where can I find a self-service restaurant?	**Dove posso trovare una tavola calda?**
Do I need to reserve a table?	**Devo riservare un tavolo?**
I'd like a table for two at nine o'clock	**Vorrei un tavolo per due alle nove, per favore**
not too near the door/the orchestra.	**non troppo vicino alla porta/all'orchestra.**
in the corner.	**nell'angolo.**
away from the kitchen.	**lontano dalla cucina.**

At the Restaurant

A table for four, please.	**Un tavolo per quattro, per favore.**
Is this our table?	**È questo il nostro tavolo?**
This table will do fine.	**Questo tavolo va bene.**
The tablecloth is dirty.	**La tovaglia è sporca.**
The table is unsteady.	**Il tavolo traballa.**
The ashtray is missing.	**Non c'è il posacenere.**
May I see the menu?	**Posso vedere il menu?**
We will have an aperitif while we look at it.	**Prendiamo un aperitivo mentre lo guardiamo.**
Please bring the wine list.	**Porti la lista dei vini, per favore.**
Have you a set menu?	**Ha un menu a prezzo fisso?**
What do you recommend today?	**Che cosa raccomanda oggi?**
What does it consist of?	**Che cos'è?**
It sounds good. I'll try it.	**Sembra buono. Io provo questo.**
The soup is cold. Please warm it up.	**La minestra è fredda. La faccia riscaldare, per favore.**
This fork is dirty. May I have a clean one?	**Questa forchetta è sporca. Posso averne una pulita?**
Will you call our waiter?	**Può chiamare il nostro cameriere?**
We did not order this.	**Non abbiamo ordinato questo piatto.**

I'd like to speak to the head waiter.	**Vorrei parlare al capo cameriere.**
My compliments to the chef.	**Complimenti al cuoco.**
It's very good.	**È molto buono.**
Have you any house wine?	**Ha del vino della casa?**
I'd like a half bottle/a carafe.	**Ne vorrei una mezza bottiglia/una caraffa.**
Which is the local wine?	**Qual'è il vino locale?**
This wine is corked.	**Questo vino sa di tappo.**
The children will share a portion.	**I bambini si divideranno una porzione.**
May we have some water?	**Posso avere dell'acqua?**
Have you any mineral water?	**Ha dell'acqua minerale?**
Have you a high chair for the child?	**Ha un seggiolone per il bambino?**
Will you please bring some cushions.	**Può portare dei cuscini.**
Where are the toilets?	**Dov'è la toilette?**

The Menu

Starters

antipasto	hors d'oeuvres
crostini alla Napoletana	fried bread with cheese and anchovies
funghi ripieni	stuffed mushrooms
frutti di mare	mixed seafood
pizza	pizza
prosciutto e melone	Parma ham and melon
pomodori ripieni	stuffed tomatoes
melanzane ripiene	stuffed aubergines
mozzarella in carrozza	bread with cheese fried in batter
risotto	rice with chicken stock
tonno e cipolle	tuna fish with onions
tortino di ricotta	cheese croquette
uova alla fiorentina	poached eggs with spinach
zucchine ripiene	stuffed baby marrows

Pastas

Most Italians start their meal with a dish of pasta and these
come in a variety of shapes. There are the long spaghetti
types, those shaped like shells, stuffed pastas and
hollow tube-like pastas. Every region has its own pasta
specialities and often a similar pasta dish appears under a
different regional name. The main gastronomic difference
between the pastas is that some of them are made at home and
some are bought from the factories. The former are vastly

superior and when restaurants advertise home-made pasta (**fatta in casa**) you are in for a treat. Other differences in pastas are that some are made with semolina, some with wheat, some have egg and the ones that look green have spinach in them. Pasta served with a sauce is called **pasta asciutta** (dry). In a consommé it is **pasta in brodo**.

cannelloni	tube-like pasta stuffed with spinach or meat
fettuccine alla marinara	noodles with tomatoes, garlic and shell-fish
gnocchi alla piemontese	little potato flour balls with sauce
gnocchi alla romana	semolina rounds with cheese
lasagne	strips of flat pasta with meat sauce
maltagliati	flat, irregularly cut pasta
maccheroni	small-tube pasta
ravioli	little pasta envelopes stuffed with spinach
spaghetti	literally 'little strings'. Spaghetti is served in a variety of ways. The two main ones are **alla napoletana**, with tomato sauce, and **alla bolognese**, with meat sauce. **Alla matriciana** is the Roman way, with bacon and tomatoes, and **alle vongole** is with cockles and tomato sauce. **Alla carbonara** is also Roman-style spaghetti, with bacon and eggs.
tagliatelle al pesto	noodles with a basil, cheese and pine nut sauce.
tortellini	small ravioli stuffed with meat.

Soups

Italians enjoy soups, especially in the mountainous areas of
the Alps and Abruzzi. Along the sea coasts fish soups are
universal. The characteristic flavour of most Italian soups is
given by the use of cheese, either grated or spread on croûtons
(**crostini**).

brodo	consommé
burrida	a Genoese fish soup
minestrone	a rich vegetable soup
minestra di pomodoro	tomato soup
pastina in brodo	small pasta in consommé
stracciatella	a Roman soup with eggs and cheese
zuppa di fagioli alla toscana	Tuscan bean soup
zuppa pavese	a consommé with egg and croûtons
zuppa di castagne	chestnut soup
zuppa di pesce	fish soup

Fish

agoni	a small sardine-sized fish found on the Italian lakes
anguilla alla ferrarese	fried eels in breadcrumbs
alici al gratin	anchovies with cheese
baccalà mantecato	creamed dried cod
calamaretti	baby inkfish
caciucco alla toscana	Tuscan fish stew

cappon magro	fish with special sauce and Melba toast
cozze al vino bianco	mussels in white wine
datteri di mare	datestone-shaped shellfish
fritto misto di mare	mixed fish fry
dentice	a Mediterranean fish
molecche	soft-shelled crabs found in Venice
polipi	octopus either served cold with oil or fried (baby octopuses are **polipetti**)
sogliole alle parmigiana	Mediterranean sole with cheese
pesce al cartoccio	fish roasted
sarde ripiene	stuffed sardines
ostriche alla veneziana	grilled oysters
scampi alla lombarda	scampi with garlic and wine
triglie alla ligure	red mullet in wine with anchovies

Meat

arista fiorentina	Florentine roast pork
abbacchio al forno o alla romana	roast sucking lamb
bollito misto	boiled meats with green sauce
braciole di vitello alla veronese	veal chops
bistecca alla pizzaiola	steak with tomato and garlic sauce
scaloppe alla bolognese	veal steaks with cheese
stufato di manzo	beef stew Genoese style

filetto di bue, ben cotto
  medio
  al sangue
	fillet steak, well done
	  medium
	  rare

lingua con olive	tongue with olives
nodini di vitello	roast veal
saltimbocca alla **romana**	veal with cheese and ham
spezzatino di vitello	veal stew
testa di vitello	calf's head
maiale al latte	pork cooked in milk
piccata al marsala	veal in Marsala wine sauce
polpettone	meat roll
ossobuco alla milanese	shin of beef with saffron rice
stracotto	beef stew
trippa alla genovese	tripe Genoese style
vitello tonnato	veal with tuna fish sauce
zampone con lenticchie	stuffed trotter of pork with lentils

Sausages

salame	salami
mortadella	a Bolognese sausage
bresaola	cured beef sliced very thin
cotechino	pork salami
zampone	pork meat stuffed into pigs' trotters

Eating and Drinking

Sauces and Styles of Cooking

alla marinara	with tomatoes and shellfish
alla bolognese	with cheese, meat and tomatoes
alla pizzaiola	with garlic, tomatoes and oregano
alla napoletana	with tomatoes
besciamella	béchamel
salsa genovese	with veal, mushrooms, wine and celery
pesto	a Genoese sauce with basil, cheese, garlic and pine nuts
salsa di fegatini	chicken liver sauce
salsa di funghi	mushroom sauce
maionese verde	green mayonnaise
allo spiedo	on a rotary grill

Game and Fowl

anitra in agrodolce	duck in sweet and sour sauce
capretto in casseruola	kid in casserole
cervo con salsa di ciliege	venison in cherry sauce
cinghiale alla cacciatora	wild boar with a ham and vegetable sauce
fagiano al madera	pheasant in Madeira sauce
lepre alla montanara	hare with pine nuts and sultanas
perniciotte alla milanese	young partridges Milan style
palombacci alla perugina	roast pigeons Perugia style

petto di pollo alla fiorentina	chicken breasts in a wine sauce
pollo in porchetta	chicken stuffed with ham
petti di tacchino alla bolognese	turkey breasts with ham, cheese and truffles
uccelletti e polenta	small birds with maize purée

Vegetables

Italians usually eat salads with their meat or accompany them with only one vegetable. Vegetables are, however, prepared as special dishes, especially in the south, where people are much poorer.

crocchette di patate	potato croquettes
cepes alla genovese	mushrooms in vine leaves
carciofi alla giudia	artichokes Jewish style
fave al prosciutto	beans and bacon
piselli al prosciutto	peas and ham
spinaci alle acciughe	spinach and anchovies
melanzane alla parmigiana	aubergines and cheese
peperonata	sweet peppers and tomatoes
verze ripiene	stuffed cabbage leaves
zucchine ripiene	stuffed marrows

Desserts

arance caramellate	caramel oranges
budino di mandorle	almond pudding

castagne al marsala	chestnuts with Marsala
crema di mascarpone	cream cheese sweetened with brandy
gelati	ice creams. An Italian speciality which has been almost overwhelmed by mass production methods. There are still places where you can get the genuine **cassata** made with cream, eggs and candied fruit and **tutti frutti**, a concoction of ice cream and a variety of fruits. Then there are the refreshing water ices, **granita**, flavoured with coffee, lemon or strawberries.
monte bianco	chestnuts and cream
pesche al vino blanco	peaches in wine
tortiglione	almond cakes
torta di albicocche	apricot tart
zabaione	egg yolks and Marsala

Drinks

Aperitifs and wine are part of the way of life of Italian people who also like mineral water. Vermouth is the most popular aperitif, either sweet (**dolce**) or dry (**secco**). Campari, a vermouth-type aperitif made with herbs, is an acquired taste. There are many kinds of Italian liqueurs from grappa, a strong grape spirit, to brandies and sweet liqueurs like Aurum and Strega.

Will you bring a Dubonnet, please?	**Può portarmi un Dubonnet, per favore?**
with ice and lemon.	**con ghiaccio e limone.**
I'd like a scotch on the rocks.	**Io vorrei uno scotch con ghiaccio.**
with soda water.	**con soda.**
with plain water.	**con acqua.**
Have you any non-alcoholic drinks?	**Ha qualcosa di non alcolico?**

Wine

Italy produces a vast quantity and variety of wines, but their classification has only recently been undertaken. This means that it is difficult to set a standard. Nevertheless the quality of the wines is often excellent. Local wines are good but they do not travel well. The following are the most important wine-growing regions.

PIEDMONT

These wines resemble the French and have much body. Barolo and Barbaresco are the best known and are made to conform to certain standards set by the organization that protects their reputation. Asti Spumante is a champagne-type white wine.

VERONA

There are some delightful wines produced near Lake Garda.
Most of them are light in body and ideal for summer
drinking. Soave is a white, Bardolino a red and the most
famous of all is Valpollicella.

EMILIA

Famous for its food, the region around Bologna, stretching as
far as Modena, also produces two good wines. Lambrusco is a
slightly sparkling red and Sangiovese a full-bodied red from
near Forli.

TUSCANY AND UMBRIA

These are great wine-producing areas, with famous names
like Chianti, a red wine, and Orvieto, a white. Almost every
village has given its name to a wine: Montepulciano, San
Gimignano, and Ruffino are just three of them.

MONTI ALBANI

The Alban hills near Rome are famous for their wines.
Frascati, a white, and Grottaferrata, a red, are two of the **vini
dei castelli**, a name that refers to the numerous castles in this
area.

NAPLES AND THE SOUTH

In Naples are the famous wines of Vesuvius, Lacrima Christi
being perhaps the most well known, and south of the bay,
near Amalfi, is the Caruso vineyard which produces a fine red
wine.

SICILY

Corvo di Salaparuta is a good Sicilian red and Marsala a
famous sweet dessert wine. Otherwise the southern wines are
thin and do not compare with those north of Rome.

Soft Drinks

May we have some tea, please?	**Potremmo avere del tè, per favore?**
a pot of tea?	**una teiera?**
a lemon tea?	**un tè al limone?**
a coffee with a drop of milk?	**un caffè macchiato?**
a coffee with milk/cream?	**un cappuccino/un caffè con panna?**
a black coffee/an iced coffee?	**un caffè nero/un caffè freddo?**
Have you any lemonade?	**Ha una limonata?**
a long, cool drink with plenty of ice?	**una grande bibita fredda con molto ghiaccio?**
an orange juice with soda water?	**una spremuta d'arancia con soda?**
a glass of cold milk?	**un bicchiere di latte freddo?**
Have you a straw?	**Ha una cannuccia?**
Do you make milk shakes?	**Fate frappés?**
Have you a bottle with a screw top?	**Ha una bottiglia con un tappo a vite?**

VOCABULARY

beef tea	**l'estratto di carne**
canned beer	**la lattina di birra**
chocolate	**il cioccolato**
cordial	**il cordiale**
cup	**la tazza**
ginger ale	**il ginger ale**
lager	**la lager**
syphon	**il sifone**
tonic water	**l'acqua tonica**
tumbler	**il bicchiere**

Shopping

Buying Food

Eating out is fun but so is buying food in the various types of food shops and markets. Italians set great store by freshness and quality, and buying food is an important operation involving discussion about the product.

At the Butcher's

What kind of meat is that?	**Che tipo di carne è questa?**
What do you call that cut?	**Come si chiama questo taglio?**
I'd like some steaks please.	**Vorrei delle bistecche, per favore.**
How much does that weigh?	**Quanto pesa?**
Will you please trim off the fat?	**Può tagliare il grasso, per piacere?**
Will you take the meat off the bone?	**Può separare la carne dall'osso?**
Will you mince it?	**Può tritarla?**
Please slice it very fine/thick.	**La tagli a fettine sottili/spesse.**
Will you chine the cutlets?	**Può levere l'osso dalle cotolette?**
I'll have a little more.	**Ne voglio ancora un pò.**
That's too much.	**Così è troppo.**
Put it in a plastic bag, please.	**La metta in una busta di plastica, per favore.**

Buying Food

Cut it in cubes.	**Lo (la) tagli a tocchetti.**

bacon	**la pancetta**
beef	**il manzo**
pot roast	**l'arrosto in casseruola**
rib	**la costa**
rump steak	**la culatta**
filet	**il filetto**
roast beef	**l'arrosto**
sirloin	**il lombo**
brains	**le cervella**
cooking fat	**il lardo**
cutlet	**la cotoletta**
escalope	**la scaloppa**
kidney	**il rognone**
lamb – shoulder/leg	**l'agnello – la spalla/il cosciotto**
liver	**il fegato**
pig's trotters	**lo zampone**
pork chops	**le braciole di maiale**
pork, leg of	**la zampa di maiale**
sausages	**le salsicce**
sweetbread	**l'animella**
tongue	**la lingua**

At the Fishmonger's

Will you clean the fish?	**Puo pulire il pesce?**
Leave/take off the head/tail/fins.	**Lasci/tolga la testa/la coda/ le pinne.**
Have you any shellfish?	**Ha dei frutti di mare?**

What is the name of that fish?   **Come si chiama questo pesce?**

VOCABULARY

anchovies	**le acciughe**
bass	**il branzino**
carp	**la carpa**
cod	**il merluzzo**
crayfish	**il gambero**
crab	**il granchio**
eel	**l'anguilla**
herring	**l'aringa**
lobster	**l'aragosta**
mullet	**la triglia**
mussels	**i molluschi**
octopus	**il polipo**
oysters	**le ostriche**
perch	**il pesce persico**
plaice	**la passera**
prawns	**i gamberi**
salmon	**il salmone**
sardines	**le sardine**
sole	**la sogliola**
squid	**i calamari**
trout	**la trota**
tunny	**il tonno**
turbot	**il rombo**
whitebait	**i pesciolini**

Buying Food

At the Delicatessen

What kind of sausages have you got?	Che tipo di salsicce avete?
I'd like a mild one/a peppery one/one without garlic.	Ne vorrei una leggera/una col pepe/una senza aglio.
May I see your selection of pâtés?	Posso vedere la vostra scelta di pâtés?
I prefer a coarse pâté/smooth pâté/game pâté.	Preferisco del pâté poco raffinato/leggero/del pâté di cacciaggione.
What is the name of that cheese?	Come si chiama quel formaggio?
Have you any goat's cheese?	Avete formaggio di capra?
Do I have to take the whole cheese or will you cut it?	Devo prendere la forma intera o lo tagliate?
May I test for ripeness?	Mi fa sentire se è maturo?
Have you any biscuits/tea biscuits?	Avete biscotti/biscotti da tè?
Do you sell breakfast cereals?	Vende cereali?
I'll take a little of each salad.	Prendo un pò d'ogni insalata.
Have you a tube of tomato purée?	Ha un tubetto di purée di pomodoro?
Have you a jar of olives?	Ha un vasetto di olive?

VOCABULARY

chitterling	le interiora
garlic sausage	la salsiccia all'aglio
ham	il prosciutto

macaroni	**i maccheroni**
olives	**le olive**
pickles	**i sottaceti**
spaghetti	**gli spaghetti**
smoked fish	**il pesce affumicato**
tinned food	**il cibo in scatola**

CHEESES

bel paese	a mild soft cheese
dolce latte	a mild version of gorgonzola
fontina	a Piedmontese cheese
gorgonzola	a blue-veined strong cheese
grana	a rich, hard sweet cheese
parmigiano	a rich, hard sweet cheese
provolone	buffalo cheese, sometimes smoked
ricotta	ewe's milk cheese

At the Greengrocer and Fruiterer's

Is the melon ripe?	**Questo melone è maturo?**
How many will make a kilo?	**Quanti fanno un chilo?**
It's for eating today/tomorrow.	**È per oggi/domani.**
Will you please weigh this bunch?	**Può pesare questo cespo?**
This lettuce is rather limp.	**Questa lattuga è un po' appassita.**
Are these apples crisp?	**Queste mele sono fresche?**
Have you got a stronger bag?	**Ha una busta più robusta?**
I will put it in my carrier.	**Lo (la) metterò nel mio carrello.**
Have you got a box?	**Ha una scatola?**

Buying Food

VOCABULARY

apples	**le mele**
apricots	**le albicocche**
asparagus	**gli asparagi**
artichokes	**i carciofi**
banana	**la banana**
beetroot	**la barbabietola**
blackberry	**la mora**
cabbage	**il cavolo**
cauliflower	**il cavolfiore**
chestnut	**la castagna**
cherry	**la ciliegia**
cress	**il crescione**
cucumber	**il cetriolo**
date	**il dattero**
fig	**il fico**
grapefruit	**il pompelmo**
grape	**l'uva**
greengage	**la susina**
hazel nut	**la nocchia**
leek	**il porro**
lemon	**il limone**
lettuce	**la lattuga**
melon	**il melone**
onions	**le cipolle**
oranges	**le arance**
pears	**le pere**
pineapple	**l'ananas**
plums	**le prugne**
potatoes	**le patate**
radishes	**i ravanelli**
raspberries	**i lamponi**
rhubarb	**il rabarbaro**
strawberries	**le fragole**
sweet corn	**il granturco**

tangerines	**i mandarini**
tomatoes	**i pomodori**
turnip	**la rapa**

AT THE GROCER

bread	**il pane**
brush	**la spazzola**
butter	**il burro**
biscuits	**i biscotti**
cereals	**i cereali**
cleaning fluid	**il liquido per lavare**
crisps	**le patatine**
detergent	**il detergente**
dried fruit	**la frutta secca**
disinfectant	**il disinfettante**
duster	**lo strofinaccio**
flour	**la farina**
jam	**la marmellata**
margarine	**la margarina**
paper napkins	**i fazzoletti di carta**
oil	**l'olio**
vinegar	**l'aceto**
washing powder	**il sapone in polvere**

Other Shops

Italian department stores are full of well-designed goods.
Best of all are the small boutiques, where the Italian flair for
the artistic is amply demonstrated. This makes shopping a
pleasure for its variety as well as for the individual character
of each establishment. Most shops are open from 0900 to
1800 hours and even later in summer.

I want to go shopping. Where are the best shops?	**Vorrei andare a fare spese.** **Dove sono i negozi migliori?**
the shops where everyone goes?	**i negozi dove vanno tutti?**
the cheaper shops?	**i negozi più economici?**
Where is the market?	**Dov'è il mercato?**
Till what time are you open?	**Fino a che ora siete aperti?**
Is there a grocer near here?	**C'è un fruttivendolo qui vicino?**

VOCABULARY

antique shop	**l'antiquario**
art gallery	**la galleria d'arte**
baker	**il panettiere**
bank	**la banca**
beauty salon	**il salone di bellezza**
bookshop	**la libreria**
butcher	**la macelleria**
chemist	**la farmacia**
confectionery	**la pasticceria**
dairy	**la latteria**
delicatessen	**la rosticceria/la salumeria**
department store	**il grande magazzino**
dry cleaner	**la tintoria**
fishmonger	**il pescivendolo**

greengrocer	**il fruttivendolo**
grocer	**il droghiere**
hairdresser	**il parrucchiere**
hardware store	**il ferramenta**
jeweller	**il gioielliere**
newsagent	**il giornalaio**
optician	**l'ottico**
photographer	**il fotografo**
shoemaker	**il calzolaio**
shoe shop	**la calzoleria**
stationer	**la cartoleria**
tailor	**il sarto**
tobacconist	**il tabaccaio**
toy shop	**il negozio di giocattoli**
travel agent	**l'agenzia di viaggi**
watchmaker	**l'orologiaio**
wine merchant	**il vinaio**

Buying Clothes

I am just looking, thank you.	**Sto solo dando un'occhiata, grazie.**
I would like to look at some shirts	**Vorrei vedere delle camicie**
plain/coloured/striped.	**tinta unita/colorate/a strisce.**
with long/short sleeves.	**con le maniche lunghe/ corte.**
in cotton.	**di cotone.**
My size is . . .	**La mia misura è . . .**
My collar/waist/chest/hip size is . . .	**La mia misura di collo/vita/ busto/fianchi è . . .**
This colour does not suit me.	**Questo colore non mi sta bene.**

87

Shopping

Have you something in red/in wool?	Ha qualcosa in rosso/in lana?
It is not my style.	Non mi piace.
I want something more casual.	Vorrei qualcosa di più portabile.
Is there a fitting room where I can try it on?	C'è un camerino dove io posso provarla?
Can I return it if it is unsuitable?	Posso restituirla se non va bene?
May I have a receipt?	Potrei avere una ricevuta?
It does not fit. It is too large/small/narrow/wide.	Non mi va bene. È troppo grande/piccola/stretta/larga.
Can you show me something else?	Può mostrarmi qualche altra cosa?
The zip is stuck/broken.	La lampo non funziona/è rotta.

VOCABULARY

MATERIALS

camel hair	la lana di cammello
chiffon	lo chiffon
cotton	il cotone
crepe	la crêpe
denim	la stoffa jeans
felt	il feltro
flannel	la flanella
gabardine	il gabardine
lace	il pizzo
leather	la pelle
linen	il lino

nylon	il nylon
piqué	il piqué
poplin	la poplina
rayon	il rayon
satin	il raso
silk	la seta
suede	la pelle scamosciata
tweed	a tela scozzese
taffeta	il taffeta
velvet	il velluto
velour	il feltro di velluto
wool	la lana
worsted	la lana filata

MEASUREMENTS

arm	braccia
leg	gamba
chest	busto
waist	vita
neck	collo
hips	fianchi
length	lunghezza

COLOURS

black	nero
blue	blu/azzurro/celeste
biscuit	biscotto
green	verde
mauve	malva
pastel colours	colori pastello
orange	arancione
red	rosso
rose	rosa
strong colours	colori forti
violet	viola
white	bianco
yellow	giallo

ITEMS OF CLOTHING

anorak	la giacca a vento
bathing hat	la cuffia da bagno
bathrobe	l'accappatoio
belt	la cintura
blazer	la giacca di flanella
blouse	la blusa
boots	gli stivali
bra	il reggiseno
briefs	le mutandine
buckle	la fibbia
button	il bottone
cap	il berretto
cardigan	il cardigan
coat	il cappotto
dinner jacket	lo smoking
dress	il vestito
elastic	l'elastico
girdle	il cinturino
gloves	i guanti
gym shoes	le scarpe da ginnastica
handkerchief	il fazzoletto
hat	il cappello
hook and eyes	i ganci
jacket	la giacca
jeans	i jeans
jumper	il maglione
negligé	il negligé
nightdress	la camicia da notte
overcoat	il soprabito
panties	le mutande
pant suit	il completo pantalone
press stud	il botone automatico
pocket	la tasca
pullover	il pullover
pyjamas	il pigiama

raincoat	**l'impermeabile**
sandals	**i sandali**
scarf	**la sciarpa**
shirt	**la camicia**
shoelaces	**i lacci da scarpa**
shoes	**le scarpe**
shorts	**i calzoncini**
skirt	**la gonna**
slip	**la sottana**
slippers	**le pantofole**
stockings	**le calze**
suit	**l'abito**
suspenders	**le giarrettiere**
swimsuit	**il costume**
thread	**il filo**
tie	**la cravatta**
tights	**la calzamaglia**
trousers	**i calzoni**
t-shirt	**la maglietta**
underpants	**le mutande**
vest	**la sottoveste**
waistcoat	**il gilè**
zip	**la chiusura lampo**

At the Shoe Shop

I want a pair of walking shoes.	**Vorrei un paio di scarpe per camminare.**
evening shoes.	**di scarpe da sera.**
moccasins.	**di mocassini.**
boots.	**un paio di stivali.**
suede shoes.	**di scarpe di camoscio.**
slippers.	**di pantofole.**
sandals.	**di sandali.**
canvas shoes.	**di scarpe di tela.**

Shopping

My size is ...	**Porto la misura ...**
I like a broad/narrow fitting.	**Le vorrei comode/giuste.**
I want shoes with high/low/flat heels.	**Vorrei delle scarpe con i tacchi alti/con i tacchi bassi/senza tacco.**
with leather soles.	**con la suola di pelle.**
with rubber soles.	**con la suola di gomma.**
with cork soles.	**con la suola di sughero.**
These are not comfortable.	**Queste non sono comode.**
May I try the other shoe?	**Posso provare anche l'altra scarpa?**
Have you got a shoe horn?	**Ha un calzascarpe?**
They are not my style.	**Non mi piacciono.**
What other colours have you got?	**Che altri colori avete?**
How much are they?	**Quanto costano?**
That is more than I want to pay.	**È più di quanto voglia spendere.**
I will wear them. Will you please wrap up my own shoes?	**Le tengo addosso. Può incartare le mie scarpe invece?**
Do you sell shoe polish/shoe cleaner/shoe brushes?	**Vendete lucido da scarpe/qualcosa per pulire le scarpe/spazzole da scarpe?**

Tobacconist

Stamps and salt can also be purchased in a tobacconist's in Italy.

A packet/carton of ... cigarettes, please.	**Un pacchetto/una stecca di ... sigarette, per piacere.**

A box of matches, please.	**Una scatola di fiammiferi.**
Do you sell English cigarettes?	**Vendete sigarette inglesi?**
What is the local brand?	**Qual'è la marca locale?**
Are they Virginian/French/Egyptian/Turkish/American tobacco?	**Sono sigarette col tabacco virginia/francese/egiziano/turco/americano?**
Have you any filter tips/king sized/menthol-cooled cigarettes?	**Avete delle sigarette con filtro/lunghe/al mentolo?**
Do you sell pipe tobacco?	**Vendete del tabacco da pipa?**
May I see your selection of pipes?	**Posso vedere la vostra scelta di pipe?**
I'd like a cigar.	**Vorrei un sigaro.**
Have you a cigar cutter?	**Ha un coltello per tagliare i sigari?**
Have you anything for cleaning a pipe?	**Ha niente per pulire le pipe?**
I'd like some snuff.	**Vorrei del tabacco da fiuto.**
Have you got any stamps?	**Avete francobolli?**
I'd like some salt, please.	**Vorrei del sale, per favore.**

VOCABULARY

box	**la scatola**
case	**l'astuccio**
cigarette lighter	**l'accendino**
cleaners	**i bastoncini per pulire le pipe**
carton	**la stecca**
flint	**la pietrina**
gas	**il gas**
lighter fluid	**la benzina**

Shopping

matches	**i fiammiferi**
packet	**il pacchetto**
pipe	**la pipa**
pouch	**la borsa del tabacco**
stamps	**i francobolli**

Hardware Stores and Electrical Goods

I'd like a heavy-duty saucepan.	**Vorrei una pentola per cucina elettrica.**
a non-stick frying pan.	**una padella col fondo che non attacchi.**
Have you a grill/charcoal?	**Ha una griglia/del carbone?**
I need a plastic/metal can for water.	**Ho bisogno di una tanica per l'acqua in plastica/in metallo.**
I'll have a bucket.	**Prenderò un secchio.**
Give me a ball of strong twine.	**Mi dia un gomitolo di corda spessa.**
I need a tow rope and a hook.	**Ho bisogno di una fune e un gancio da rimorchio.**
I need a battery for my torch/radio.	**Ho bisogno di una pila per la mia lampada/per la mia radio.**

VOCABULARY

adaptor	**il trasformatore**
basket	**il cestino**
battery	**la pila**
brush	**la spazzola**
bulb	**la lampadina**

94

car radio	**la radio della macchina**
chamois leather	**la pelle di camoscio**
distilled water	**l'acqua distillata**
duster	**lo straccio/lo strofinaccio**
fork	**la forchetta**
hammer	**il martello**
insulating tape	**il nastro isolante**
knife	**il coltello**
mallet	**il maglio**
penknife	**il temperino**
percolator	**il filtro**
plug	**la spina**
saw	**la sega**
scissors	**le forbici**
screwdriver	**il cacciavite**
shaver	**il rasoio**
spoon	**il cucchiaio**
string	**lo spago**
tweezers	**le pinze**
wire	**il filo**
wrench	**la chiave inglese**

Chemist's

Do I need a doctor's prescription?	**Ho bisogno di una ricetta?**
Is there an all-night chemist open?	**C'è qualque farmacia aperta tutta la notte?**
Can you make up this prescription?	**Può darmi questo preparato?**
When will it be ready?	**Quando sarà pronto?**
Will you write down the instructions, in English if possible?	**Può scrivere le istruzioni, in inglese, possibilmente?**

Shopping

Is this safe for children?	**Va bene per i bambini?**
Have you anything for a cold/sore throat/cough?	**Avete qualcosa contro il raffreddore/mal di gola/la tosse?**
I'd like to buy a thermometer.	**Vorrei un termometro.**
Would you please have a look at this cut/bruise?	**Può dare un'occhiata a questo taglio/a questa contusione?**
What kind of bandage would be best?	**Che tipo di benda suggerisce?**
I've got diarrhoea.	**Ho la diarrea.**
an upset stomach.	**mal di stomaco.**
indigestion.	**fatto indigestione.**
a headache.	**mal di testa.**
sunburn.	**una scottatura da sole.**
I am constipated.	**Sono costipato(a).**

VOCABULARY

aspirin	**l'aspirina**
antibiotics	**gli antibiotici**
bandage	**la benda**
band-aids	**il cerotto**
contraceptive	**il contraccettivo**
corn plaster	**il callifugo**
cough mixture	**lo sciroppo per la tosse**
cough lozenges	**le pastiglie per la tosse**
cotton wool	**l'ovatta**
disinfectant	**il disinfettante**
ear drops	**le gocce per le orecchie**
gargle	**i gargarismi**
gauze	**la garza**

insect repellant	**l'insetticida**
iodine	**lo iodio**
iron pills	**le pillole con ferro**
laxative	**il lassativo**
lip salve	**la pomata per le labbra**
sanitary towels	**gli assorbenti**
sedative	**il sedativo**
sleeping pill	**il sonnifero**
tranquillizers	**i tranquillanti**
thermometer	**il termometro**
vitamins	**le vitamine**

TOILET ARTICLES

after shave	**il dopobarba**
astringent	**l'astringente**
bath salts	**i sali da bagno**
bath oil	**l'olio da bagno**
cologne	**la colonia**
cream:	**la crema:**
cleansing	**detergente**
cuticle	**per le unghie**
foundation	**fondotinta**
moisturising	**idratante**
deodorant	**il deodorante**
emery boards	**le limette di cartavetro**
eye pencil	**la matita per gli occhi**
eye shadow	**l'ombretto**
face pack	**la maschera per il viso**
face powder	**la cipria**
lipstick	**il rossetto**
nailbrush	**lo spazzolino per le unghie**
nailfile	**la lima per le unghie**
nail polish	**lo smalto**
nail polish remover	**l'acetone**
perfume	**il profumo**
rouge	**il rosso per le guance**
safety pins	**le spille di sicurezza**

Shopping

shampoo	**lo shampoo**
shaving cream	**la crema da barba**
shaving brush	**il pennello da barba**
soap	**il sapone**
suntan oil	**l'unguente solare**
sponge	**la spugna**
tissues	**i fazzoletti di carta**
toilet paper	**la carta igienica**
tooth paste	**il dentifricio**
tooth brush	**lo spazzolino da denti.**

At the Photographer's

I'd like to buy a camera.	**Vorrei comprare una macchina fotografica.**
One that is cheap and easy to use.	**Una economica e facile da usare.**
Will you please check my camera?	**Può controllare la mia macchina?**
The film gets stuck.	**La pellicola si blocca.**
The exposure meter is not working.	**L'esposimetro non funziona.**
The flash does not light up.	**Il flash non funziona.**
The film winder is jammed.	**La leva che fa girare la pellicola è bloccata.**
Can you do it soon?	**Può aggiustarla subito?**
Will you please process this film?	**Può sviluppare la pellicola?**
I want some black-and-white/ colour film.	**Vorrei una pellicola in bianco e nero/a colori.**

98

Is this film for use in daylight or artificial light?	**Questa pellicola va bene con la luce del giorno o con la luce artificiale?**
I need a light meter.	**Vorrei un esposimetro.**
How much is an electronic flash?	**Quanto costa un flash elettronico?**

VOCABULARY

Films 120, 127, 135, 620	**Pellicole centoventi, centoventisette, centotrentacinque, seicentoventi.**
20 exposures	**venti pose**
36 exposures	**trentasei pose**
a fast film	**una pellicola ad impressione veloce**
a fine-grain film	**una pellicola a grana sottile**
cine film 8 mm/16 mm	**un film otto/sedici millimetri.**
flash bulbs	**le lampadine per il flash**
lens	**la lente**
lens cap	**il coperchio della lente**
red filter	**il filtro rosso**
yellow filter	**il filtro giallo**
ultra violet	**ultravioletto**
range finder	**la messa a fuoco**
shutter	**l'otturatore**
long-focus lens	**il teleobbiettivo**
wide-angle lens	**il grandangolo**
camera case	**la custodia**

Bookshop/Stationer's

On which shelf are the books on art/history/politics/sport?	**In quale scaffale sono i libri d'arte/storici/politici/ di sport?**

Shopping

Where are the guide books?	**Dove sono le guide?**
I want a pocket dictionary.	**Vorrei un vocabolario tascabile.**
Have you any English newspapers?	**Ha giornali inglesi?**
Have you any English paperbacks?	**Ha libri inglesi in edizione economica?**
Can you recommend an easy-to-read book in Italian?	**Può consigliarmi un libro facile da leggere in italiano?**
Do you sell second-hand books?	**Vendete libri di seconda mano?**
I want a map of the area.	**Vorrei una cartina della zona.**
The scale of this one is too small.	**La scala di questa è troppo piccola.**
Have you got refills for this ballpoint pen?	**Ha un ricambio per questa penna a sfera?**
Can you please deliver the English newspaper every morning?	**Potrebbe mandarmi a casa ogni mattina il giornale inglese?**

VOCABULARY

address book	**l'agenda**
box of crayons	**la scatola di colori**
carbon paper	**la carta carbone**
cellophane	**lo Scotch**
drawing paper	**la carta da disegno**
drawing pins	**le puntine da disegno**
envelopes	**le buste**
exercise book	**il quaderno**

fountain pen	**la penna stilografica**
greaseproof paper	**la carta oleata**
glue	**la colla**
ink	**l'inchiostro**
label	**la targhetta**
notebook	**il taccuino**
notepaper	**la carta da lettera**
paste	**la colla**
pen	**la penna**
pencil	**la matita**
pencil sharpener	**il temperamatite**
playing cards	**le carte da gioco**
rubber	**la gomma**
ruler	**la regola**
silver foil	**la carta argentata**
typewriter ribbon	**il nastro per la macchina da scrivere**
typing paper	**la carta per la macchina da scrivere**
writing pad	**il blocco**

Buying Souvenirs

Are all these things made in Italy?	**Queste cose sono fatte in Italia?**
This is a nice straw hat.	**Questo è un bel cappello di paglia.**
I like this bag.	**Mi piace questa borsa.**
Have you any costume jewellery?	**Avete gioielli fantasia?**
I'm looking for bracelet charms.	**Sto cercando un bracciale portafortuna.**
I'd like to try on that ring.	**Vorrei provare questo anello.**

Shopping

What is the bracelet made of?	**Di che cosa è fatto questo bracciale?**
I collect copper ware. Have you any pots?	**Colleziono oggetti di rame. Avete dei vasi?**
I'd like some local pottery.	**Vorrei della terracotta del luogo.**
Can you pack this carefully?	**Può incartarlo(la) per bene?**
Do you despatch things abroad?	**Spedite oggetti all'estero?**
I'm just looking around.	**Sto solo dando un'occhiata.**
I will come back later.	**Tornerò più tardi.**
Can I leave a deposit on it and return tomorrow?	**Posso dare un anticipo per questo e tornare domani?**
Do you take foreign cheques with a Eurocard?	**Accettate assegni in valuta straniera con una Eurocard?**

Vocabulary

beads	**le perline**
brooch	**la spilla**
chain	**la catena**
cigarette lighter	**l'accendino**
clock	**l'orologio**
cufflinks	**i bottoni gemelli**
earrings	**gli orecchini**
jewel box	**la scatola per i gioielli**
music box	**la scatola armonica**
necklace	**la collana**
rosary	**il rosario**
silverware	**l'argento**
watchstrap	**il cinturino per l'orologio**
wristwatch	**l'orologio da polso**

Entertainment

Out for the Evening

Nightclubs

Can you recommend a nightclub with a good show?	Può consigliarmi un nightclub con un bello spettacolo?
a place with dancing and cabaret?	un posto dove si balli e ci sia il cabaret?
a disco?	una discoteca?
an open-air dance?	un locale dove si balli all'aperto?
a nightclub with hostesses?	un night con hostesses?
Is there an entrance fee?	Si paga il biglietto per entrare?
Does it include drinks?	Sono incluse le consumazioni?
What is the cost of drinks?	Quanto costa una consumazione?
At what time does the show start?	A che ora comincia lo spettacolo?
Is there a different price for drinks at the bar?	Il prezzo è differente, se si beve al bar?
I do not want a photograph.	Non voglio fotografie.

Theatre/Opera

Is there a ticket agency near?	C'è un botteghino del teatro qui vicino?
Is there another way of getting a ticket?	C'è qualche altro modo per avere un biglietto?

103

Entertainment

Are there any last-minute returns?	**Ci sono biglietti dell'ultimo minuto?**
Are there tickets available on the black market?	**Ci sono biglietti disponibili al mercato nero?**
Do I have to wear evening dress?	**Devo mettere un vestito da sera?**
I'd like a souvenir programme.	**Vorrei un programma per ricordo.**
What is the name of the prima donna?	**Come si chiama la prima donna?**
Who is the leading actor?	**Chi è il primo attore?**
How long is the interval?	**Quanto dura l'intervallo?**
Where is the bar?	**Dov'è il bar?**

Vocabulary

applause	**l'applauso**
audience	**il pubblico**
baritone	**il baritono**
bass	**il basso**
composer	**il compositore**
conductor	**il direttore d'orchestra**
contralto	**il contralto**
encore	**il bis**
orchestra	**l'orchestra**
playwright	**l'autore drammatico**
scenery	**lo scenario**
soprano	**il soprano**
stage	**il palcoscenico**
tenor	**il tenore**

Cinema

What is on at the cinema?	**Che cosa c'è al cinema?**
Have you got a guide to what's on?	**Dove posso trovare un programma dei cinema?**
Two tickets for the stalls/circle, please.	**Due biglietti per la platea/ per la galleria, per favore.**
Will we have to queue for long?	**Dovremo fare una lunga fila?**
I want a seat near the front/at the back/in the middle.	**Vorrei un posto davanti/ dietro/nel mezzo.**
Do I tip the usherette?	**Devo dare una mancia alla maschera?**
I'd rather sit over there.	**Preferirei sedermi là.**
Will you please shine your torch here?	**Può farmi luce in questo punto?**
I have dropped something.	**Ho fatto cadere qualcosa.**
Is there an ice cream seller?	**Si vendono gelati?**
At what time does the film start?	**A che ora comincia il film?**
Will you please move over to the right/left.	**Può spostarsi sulla destra/ sulla sinistra, per favore.**
Can you please remove your hat?	**Può levarsi il cappello, per favore?**

<small>VOCABULARY</small>

actor	**l'attore**
actress	**l'attrice**
director	**il regista**

Entertainment

dubbing	**il doppiaggio**
interval	**l'intervallo**
producer	**il produttore**
projector	**il proiettore**
screen	**lo schermo**
sound	**il suono**
star	**la diva/la stella**

Concert Hall

I want a seat from which I can see the pianist's hands.	**Vorrei un posto da dove possa vedere le mani del pianista.**
Can I buy the score?	**È possibile comprare la partitura?**
Who is conducting tonight?	**Chi dirige l'orchestra stasera?**
Who is the soloist?	**Chi è il solista?**

bass	**il basso**
bassoon	**il fagotto**
brass	**gli ottoni**
cello	**il violoncello**
clarinet	**il clarinetto**
cymbals	**i cimbali**
drum	**il tamburo/la batteria**
french horn	**il cornetto**
flute	**il flauto**
percussion	**le percussioni**
saxophone	**il sassofono**
strings	**le corde**

timpani	**i timpani**
trombone	**il trombone**
trumpet	**la tromba**
violin	**il violino**
wind	**i fiati**

Casino

What games are played here?	**Quali tipi di gioco si fanno qui?**
Is there a minimum stake in this room?	**C'è una puntata minima in questa sala?**
Can I buy some chips?	**Vorrei delle fiches.**
I should like 20,000 lire worth.	**Vorrei ventimila lire in fiches.**
Excuse me, those are my chips.	**Scusi, ma queste sono le mie fiches.**
I'll take another card.	**Prenderò un'altra carta.**
No more.	**Basta.**
Pass me the dice please.	**Mi passi i dadi, per favore.**

VOCABULARY

ace	**l'asso**
bet	**la scommessa**
blackjack	**blackjack**
cards	**le carte**
chemin de fer	**chemin de fer**
clubs	**i fiori**
craps	**craps**
croupier	**il croupier**

Entertainment

diamonds	**i quadri**
evens	**pari**
hearts	**i cuori**
jack	**il fante**
joker	**il jolly**
king	**il re**
poker	**il poker**
queen	**la donna**
spades	**i picche**

Out for the Day

On the Beach

Does one have to pay to use this beach?	**Questa è una spiaggia a pagamento?**
Is there a free section of the beach?	**C'è una spiaggia libera?**
Is it clean?	**È pulita?**
How much does it cost per day/per week to hire a cabin?	**Quanto costa prendere in affitto al giorno/a settimana una cabina?**
a deckchair?	**una sedia a sdraio?**
air mattress?	**un materassino di gomma?**
sun umbrella?	**un ombrellone?**
Can I leave valuables in the cabin?	**Posso lasciare cose di valore in cabina?**
Is the ticket valid all day?	**Il biglietto è valido per tutta la giornata?**
Does the beach shelve steeply?	**Il mare è profondo vicino alla spiaggia?**
Is it safe for swimming?	**È sicuro per nuotare?**
Are there any currents?	**Ci sono delle correnti?**
Is it safe to dive off the rocks?	**È sicuro tuffarsi dalle rocce?**
Where is the freshwater shower?	**Dov'è la doccia con l'acqua fredda?**
Have you any tar remover?	**Ha niente per levare il catrame?**

On the Beach

Can I hire a swimsuit?	**Posso prendere in affitto un costume da bagno?**
I've cut my foot. Have you any elastoplast?	**Mi sono tagliato un piede. Ha un cerotto?**
Is there a lost property office?	**C'è un ufficio oggetti smarriti?**
Is there a children's beach club?	**C'è un club per i bambini nella spiaggia?**
At what time are the keep fit classes?	**A che ora ci sono le classi di ginnastica?**
Is there water ski tuition available?	**È possibile fare lezioni di sci d'acqua?**
Does it matter if I can't swim?	**Ha importanza se non so nuotare?**
Where is the nearest beach shop?	**Dov'è il più vicino negozio di articoli da spiaggia?**
Have you got a life jacket?	**Ha un giubbotto salvagente?**
Is this a good place for skin diving?	**È un buon posto questo per nuotare sott'acqua?**
Help! I'm in difficulty.	**Aiuto! Sono in difficoltà.**

VOCABULARY

beach ball	**il pallone gonfiabile**
cactus	**il cactus**
goggles	**gli occhiali subacquei**
harpoon gun	**il rampone**
high tide	**l'alta marea**
lilo	**il materassino gonfiabile**
low tide	**la bassa marea**
net	**la rete**

promenade	**la passeggiata**
pedalo	**il moschone a pedali**
pines	**i pini**
raft	**la zattera**
rocks	**le rocce**
rowing boat	**la barca a remi**
sand	**la sabbia**
sandals	**i sandali**
sea	**il mare**
seaweed	**le alghe**
shells	**le conchiglie**
shingle	**i ciottoli**
sun oil	**l'olio solare**
surf	**la risacca**
surf board	**l'acquaplano**
underwater	**sott'acqua**
waterski instructor	**l'istruttore di sci d'acqua**
yacht	**lo yacht**

Sightseeing

Where can I get a good guide book?	**Dove posso trovare una buona guida?**
Is there an excursion round the city?	**C'è qualche escursione della città?**
Is it a conducted party?	**È un gruppo con accompagnatore?**
Am I allowed to go round alone?	**Posso andarmene in giro da solo?**
Where do I find an official guide?	**Dove posso trovare una guida autorizzata?**
Does the whole day excursion include lunch?	**Il pranzo è incluso nel giorno di escursione?**

Sightseeing

Are the entrance fees extra?	**I biglietti d'entrata sono extra?**
Should I tip the guide/driver?	**Devo dare la mancia alla guida/all'autista?**
I'd like to stay here longer.	**Vorrei restare qui più a lungo.**
I'll meet the party later.	**Raggiungerò il gruppo più tardi.**
Where will you be?	**Dove sarete?**
Will you please write it down?	**Può scrivermelo?**
Can I hire an audioguide?	**È possibile prendere in affitto un' audioguida?**

In Churches

Do ladies have to cover their heads?	**Le signore si devono coprire la testa?**
Is it all right to enter like this?	**Possiamo entrare così?**
How old is this church?	**Di quale epoca è questa chiesa?**
Who founded it?	**Chi l'ha fondata?**
Are the stained glass windows original?	**Quei vetri istoriati sono autentici?**
Can one illuminate the fresco?	**È possibile illuminare l'affresco?**
Is one allowed to go up the bell tower?	**Si può salire sul campanile?**
Is there a book about the church?	**C'è qualche libro sulla chiesa?**

May I leave a small contribution?

Posso fare un'offerta?

VOCABULARY

abbey	l'abbazia
aisles	le navate
altar	l'altare
arch	l'arco
basilica	la basilica
candle	la candela
cathedral	la cattedrale
chapel	la cappella
cloister	il chiostro
crucifix	il crocifisso
crypt	la cripta
convent	il convento
choir	il coro
column	la colonna
fresco	l'affresco
font	il fonte battesimale
monastery	il monastero
nave	la navata centrale
rood	la croce
sculpture	la scultura
shrine	il santuario
west front	la facciata

Art Galleries and Museums

Have you a catalogue?

Ha un catalogo?

Have you an illustrated catalogue?

Ha un catalogo illustrato?

Are there any plaster casts?

Ci sono sculture?

Sightseeing

Do you sell transparencies?	**Vendete diapositive?**
Am I allowed to photograph?	**È permesso fare delle fotografie?**
May I use my tripod?	**Posso usare il cavalletto?**
Is the gallery open on Sunday?	**La galleria d'arte è aperta di Domenica?**
Is it free?	**È gratis?**
Where can I find the Dutch School?	**Dove posso trovare la Scuola Olandese?**
Do you make photocopies?	**Fate fotocopie?**
Where is the library?	**Dov'è la biblioteca?**

Vocabulary

antique books	**i libri antichi**
bas relief	**i bassorilievi**
china	**le ceramiche**
costumes	**i costumi**
drawing	**il disegno**
engraving	**l'incisione**
etching	**l'acquaforte**
frame	**la cornice**
furniture	**i mobili**
jewellery	**i gioielli**
lithograph	**la litografia**
miniature	**la miniatura**
porcelain	**la porcellana**
pottery	**la ceramica**
silverware	**l'argenteria**

Historical Sights

Will there be far to walk?	**C'è molto da camminare?**
Can I wait here till you return?	**Posso aspettarvi qui?**
Is there a souvenir stall?	**C'è una bancarella di souvenirs?**
Where can we get a cold drink?	**Dove si può trovare una bibita fresca?**
Is there a plan of the grounds?	**C'è una mappa del luogo?**
I would like to walk round the gardens.	**Vorrei fare un giro nei giardini.**

VOCABULARY

arena	**l'arena**
aqueduct	**l'acquedotto**
amphitheatre	**l'anfiteatro**
armour	**l'armatura**
battlements	**i bastioni**
catacombs	**le catacombe**
cannon	**il cannone**
castle	**il castello**
courtyard	**il cortile**
column	**la colonna**
crossbow	**la balestra**
fort	**il forte**
forum	**il foro**
fountain	**la fontana**
fortifications	**la fortificazione**
gate	**il cancello**
pediment	**il frontone**
portcullis	**la saracinesca**

Sightseeing

viaduct	**il viadotto**
walls	**le mura**

Gardens

Are these gardens open to the public?	**Sono aperti al pubblico questi giardini?**
Can we walk where we like?	**Si può camminare da tutte le parti?**
How long will it take to walk around?	**Quanto tempo ci vuole per fare il giro?**
At what time do you close?	**A che ora chiude?**
Is there a plan of the gardens?	**C'è una mappa dei giardini?**
Where is the greenhouse/ tropical plant house?	**Dov'è la serra/la serra delle piante tropicali?**
May we sit on the grass?	**Ci si può sedere sul prato?**
What is the name of that plant/ flower?	**Come si chiama quella pianta/quel fiore?**
Is there a lake/a pond?	**C'è un lago/uno stagno?**
Who designed these gardens?	**Chi ha disegnato questi giardini?**

VOCABULARY

ash	**il frassino**
beech	**il faggio**
birch	**la betulla**
bougainvillea	**la bougainville**
clematis	**la clematide**
carnation	**il garofano**

cherry	**il ciliegio**
chrysanthemum	**il crisantemo**
daffodil	**l'asfodelo**
dahlia	**la dalia**
daisy	**la margherita**
deciduous tree	**l'albero deciduo**
elm	**l'olmo**
evergreen	**il sempreverde**
fir	**l'abete**
geranium	**il geranio**
herbaceous border	**l'aiuola**
ivy	**l'edera**
lily	**il giglio**
moss	**il muschio**
nasturtium	**il nasturzio**
oak	**la quercia**
plane	**il platano**
pear	**il pero**
pine	**il pino**
poplar	**il pioppo**
rose	**la rosa**
tulip	**il tulipano**
violet	**la violetta**
wisteria	**la glicine**

The Zoo

The children would like to visit the zoo.	**I bambini vorrebbero andare allo zoo.**
Is it open every day?	**È aperto tutti i giorni?**
Is there a nature reserve?	**C'è un parco naturale?**
Can one drive through it?	**Si può attraversare in macchina?**

Sightseeing

Where can we park the car?	**Dove si può parcheggiare la macchina?**
Where can one buy animal food?	**Dove si può comprare del cibo per animali?**
When is feeding time?	**Quand'è l'ora del pasto?**
Is there an insect house?	**C'è una casa degli insetti?**
Can the children ride an elephant?	**I bambini possono andare sull'elefante?**
Is there a children's zoo?	**C'è uno zoo per i bambini?**

VOCABULARY

aquarium	**l'acquario**
ants	**le formiche**
antelope	**l'antilope**
bird	**l'uccello**
bison	**il bisonte**
baboon	**il babbuino**
bat	**il pipistrello**
cat	**il gatto**
dog	**il cane**
crocodile	**il coccodrillo**
frog	**la rana**
giraffe	**la giraffa**
hippopotamus	**l'ippopotamo**
horse	**il cavallo**
hyena	**la iena**
leopard	**il leopardo**
lion	**il leone**
parrot	**il pappagallo**
rhinoceros	**il rinoceronte**
seal	**la foca**
snake	**il serpente**

118

| turtle | **la tartaruga** |
| zebra | **la zebra** |

Sport

One of the truly Italian sports is motor racing which is
followed with great enthusiasm. The famous motor racing
track at Monza is near Milan and a hair-raising drive round
Sicily is called the Targa Florio. The most popular sports are
football and cycling. Italians also play tennis and golf and
they are keen fishermen and enjoy rough shooting.

Football

Where is the stadium?	**Dov'è lo stadio?**
How does one get there?	**Come ci si arriva?**
Should I book tickets?	**Bisogna riservare i biglietti?**
Will it be very crowded?	**Sarà molto affollato?**
Who is playing?	**Chi gioca?**
Is there a local team?	**C'è una squadra locale?**
I want a ticket for the main stand/under cover/in the open.	**Vorrei un biglietto per la tribuna principale/al coperto/allo scoperto.**
May I have a programme?	**Posso avere un programma?**

VOCABULARY

attack	**l'attacco**
area	**l'area**
football (ball)	**il pallone**
football (game)	**il calcio**
defence	**la difesa**
goalkeeper	**il portiere**
goal posts	**i pali**
halfway line	**la linea di mezzo**

Sport

linesmen	**i guardalinea**
penalty area	**l'area di rigore**
players	**i giocatori**
referee	**l'arbitro**
team	**la squadra**

Race Meeting

I want a ticket for the paddock/a grandstand seat, please.	**Voglio un biglietto per il galoppatoio/un posto in tribuna, per favore.**
Where can I place a bet?	**Dove posso fare una puntata?**
What are the odds on number 5?	**A quanto è dato il numero cinque?**
I'd like to back it to win/each way/for a place.	**Vorrei puntarlo vincente/in ogni modo/piazzato.**
Which is the favourite?	**Chi è il favorito?**
I will back the outsider.	**Punterò sul cavallo meno favorito.**
Is the jockey well known?	**Il fantino è famoso?**

VOCABULARY

course	**il terreno**
filly	**la puledra**
flat	**piano**
horse	**il cavallo**
hurdles	**gli ostacoli**
jockey	**il fantino**
owner	**il proprietario**

photo finish	**il photo-finish**
rails	**le sbarre**
stable	**la scuderia**
starting gate	**la barriera di partenza**
tote	**il totip**
trainer	**l'allenatore**

Tennis

Is there a tennis club near here?	**C'è un campo da tennis qui vicino?**
Where is the championship being held?	**Dove si svolge il campionato?**
How can I get tickets?	**Come posso procurarmi alcuni biglietti?**
Should I arrive early?	**Devo arrivare presto?**
Who is playing?	**Chi gioca?**
Is it on hard courts or grass?	**È su campo battuto o d'erba?**
I want to watch the men's singles/the doubles/mixed doubles.	**Voglio vedere le partite maschili/i doppi/i doppi misti.**
How do you score in Italian?	**Come si contano i punti in italiano?**
15, 30, 40, deuce, advantage in/out, game, set, match.	**Quindici, trenta, quaranta, quaranta-quaranta, vantaggio dentro/fuori, gioco, set, partita.**
Shall we toss for service?	**Decidiamo con una moneta per il servizio?**
Let's adjust the net.	**Regoliamo la rete.**

Sport

It's too high/too low.	**È troppo alta/troppo bassa.**
That was out/in/on the line.	**Quella era fuori/dentro/sulla linea.**
Good shot.	**Bel colpo.**
Will you keep the score.	**Tiene Lei il punteggio?**
Change ends.	**Cambiare campo.**

VOCABULARY

backhand	**il rovescio**
forehand	**il dritto**
racquet	**la racchetta**
rally	**il palleggio**
smash	**la schiacciata**
spin	**il tiro con effetto**
tennis ball	**la palla da tennis**
umpire	**l'arbitro**
volley	**la volata**

Golf

Is there a golf course nearby?	**C'è un campo da golf qui vicino?**
Does one have to be a member?	**Bisogna essere membro?**
Is there temporary membership?	**È possibile iscriversi temporaneamente?**
How much does it cost to play?	**Quanto costa giocare?**
I'd like a caddy.	**Vorrei un portamazze.**
Are there any trolleys for hire?	**Si possono affittare dei carrelli?**

I'd like to speak to the professional.	**Vorrei parlare con un istruttore.**
Are you free for lessons?	**Ha tempo per darmi delle lezioni?**
Will you play a round with me?	**Vuole giocare una partita con me?**
My handicap is eighteen.	**Il mio handicap è la diciottesima.**
My problem is a slice/hook.	**Il mio problema è la slice/ l'hook.**
I can't get any length on my drive.	**Non riesco a fare un lancio lungo con il mio tiro.**
My approach shots are weak.	**I miei tiri di avvicinamento sono deboli.**
I'll do some putting while I wait for you.	**Farò un pò di buche mentre l'aspetto.**
Can I hire some clubs?	**Posso affittare alcune mazze?**
May I have a scorecard?	**Posso avere un foglio per il punteggio?**

VOCABULARY

bunker	**l'ostacolo**
birdie	**birdie**
club house	**il circolo del golf**
eagle	**eagle**
fairway	**il percorso regolare**
golf bag	**la borsa da golf**
green	**il prato**
irons	**le mazze di ferro**

Sport

mashie	**il mashie**
niblick	**il niblick**
par	**pari**
the rough	**l'erba alta**
tee	**tee**

Water-Skiing

I have never skiied before, not even on snow.	**Non ho mai sciato prima d'ora, neanche sulla neve.**
I am not a good swimmer.	**Non so nuotare bene.**
Do I wear a life jacket?	**Devo indossare una giacca salvagente?**
Will you please help me to put on the skis?	**Mi può aiutare a mettermi sullo sci?**
Please pass me the rope.	**Mi passi la corda, per favore.**
May I ride on the speed boat?	**Posso andare sul motoscafo?**
Can I borrow a wetsuit?	**Posso prendere in prestito una tuta?**
I'm ready now.	**Sono pronto(a) ora.**
Just a moment.	**Un momento solo.**

VOCABULARY

aquaplane	**l'acquaplano**
bathing hat	**la cuffia da bagno**
goggles	**gli occhiali subacquei**
jump	**il salto**
monoski	**il monosci**
slalom	**lo slalom**

Riding

Is there a riding stable in the area?	C'è un galoppatoio nella zona?
Can I hire a horse for riding?	Posso affittare un cavallo per cavalcare?
Do you give lessons?	Date lezioni?
I'd like to go on a hack.	Vorrei andare su un cavallo da nolo.
I want a quiet horse.	Voglio un cavallo tranquillo.
Have you any ponies?	Avete ponies?
Will an instructor accompany the ride?	Ci accompagnerà un istruttore?
I'd like to practise jumping.	Vorrei esercitarmi nel salto.
I am an experienced rider/a novice.	Sono un esperto cavallerizzo/ un' esperta cavallerizza/ inesperto(a).
Do you have English saddles?	Ha delle selle inglesi?
This horse has gone lame.	Questo cavallo si è azzoppato.
The girth is too loose.	Il sottopancia è troppo lento.
Will you please adjust my stirrups?	Può sistemarmi le staffe, per piacere?
Will you hold my horse while I get on?	Può tenere il cavallo mentre salgo?
Will you give me a leg-up?	Può aiutarmi a salire?

Sport

Vocabulary

bit	il morso
blinkers	i paraocchi
bridle	la briglia
harness	i finimenti
hoof	lo zoccolo
hock	il garretto
mare	la puledra
reins	le redini
stallion	lo stallone
withers	il garrese

Fishing

Where can I get a permit?	**Dove si può ottenere una licenza di pesca?**
Is there fishing in this area?	**Si può pescare in questa zona?**
Are there any trout or salmon?	**Ci sono trote o salmoni?**
How much does a day's fishing cost?	**Quanto costa pescare per un giorno?**
Is that per rod?	**Costa così per ogni canna da pesca?**
Where can I get some bait?	**Dove posso trovare delle esche?**
Is there a minimum size that I am allowed to keep?	**C'è un limite minimo di grandezza per i pesci che è permesso tenere?**
What is the best time of day to go out?	**Qual'è l'ora migliore per andare a pesca?**

Are there any boats that will take me deep sea fishing?	**Ci sono barche disponibili per la pesca d'alto mare?**
Do they provide tackle?	**Forniscono gli attrezzi?**

VOCABULARY

fishing season	**la stagione di pesca**
fly	**la mosca**
float	**il galleggiante**
gaff	**l'uncino**
hook	**l'amo**
line	**la lenza**
lure	**l'esca**
net	**la rete**
reel	**il gomitolo**
spinner	**il mulinello**
weights	**i piombini**

Shooting

Where can I shoot?	**Dove posso sparare?**
Do I need a licence?	**Serve una licenza?**
I'd like to borrow a 12-bore shotgun.	**Vorrei prendere in prestito un fucile da caccia calibro dodici.**
I have my own rifle.	**Ho il mio fucile.**
Is there a shooting party I could join?	**C'è una partita di caccia a cui posso aggregarmi?**
Is there a clay pigeon shoot?	**C'è un campo di tiro al piccione artificiale?**

Sport

Is there a rifle range near?	**C'è un poligono nelle vicinanze?**
When does the season for chamois begin?	**Quando comincia la stagione del camoscio?**

Vocabulary

barrel	**la canna**
backsight	**il mirino posteriore**
bullets	**le pallottole**
butt	**il calcio**
catch	**la preda**
cartridges	**le cartucce**
ejector	**l'espulsore**
foresight	**il mirino**
hammer	**il cane**
revolver	**la rivoltella**
safety catch	**la sicura**
trigger	**il grilletto**
telescopic sight	**il mirino telescopico**

Sailing and Boating

I'd like to hire a dinghy.	**Vorrei affittare una piccola imbarcazione.**
Is an outboard motor extra?	**Il motore fuoribordo è extra?**
Does this have an auxiliary engine?	**Ha un motore ausiliario?**
How many berths are there?	**Quanti posti letto ci sono?**
How much water does it draw?	**Quanta acqua ci va?**

Is there a stove/sink/chemical toilet?	C'è un forno/lavandino/w.c. (*voo-chee*) chimico?
Are all cutlery, china and cooking utensils included?	Sono incluse le posate, le stoviglie e gli utensili da cucina?
Are sheets and blankets provided?	Fornite lenzuola e coperte?
Have you got a map of the river?	Ha una cartina del fiume?
Are there many locks to negotiate?	Bisogna attraversare molte chiuse?
At what time do the locks close?	A che ora chiudono le chiuse?
How far is it to the next place where I can get some fuel?	Quanto dista il prossimo posto dove posso fare rifornimento?
Can I leave the boat here while we go to the shops?	Posso lasciare la barca qui mentre andiamo ai negozi?
Where is the next refuse dump?	Dov'è il prossimo posto per buttare i rifiuti?
Will you please give me a tow?	Mi può trainare, per favore?

VOCABULARY

anchor	l'ancora
boat	la barca
boathook	il gancio d'accosto
bow	la prua
canoe	la canoa
chart	la carta nautica
diesel engine	il motore diesel
deck	il ponte

Sport

fenders	**i parabordo**
halyards	**la sagola**
hull	**lo scafo**
jib	**il fiocco**
keel	**la chiglia**
lifebelt	**la cintura salvagente**
lifejacket	**il giubbotto salvagente**
mainsail	**la vela maestra**
mast	**l'albero maestro**
motor boat	**la barca a motore**
paddle	**il remo**
pennant	**la fiamma**
port (left)	**il babordo (sinistra)**
propeller	**il propulsore**
rowing boat	**la barca a remi**
sail	**la vela**
sheets	**le scotte**
starboard (right)	**il tribordo (destra)**
to steer	**governare**
stern	**la poppa**
tiller	**la barra del timone**
yacht	**lo yacht**

Winter Sports

The region where Italy and France and Switzerland meet is
crowned by some of the highest Alps and a variety of ski
resorts, from the large, traditional ones found in the Val
d'Aosta to ultra-modern complexes. In the Dolomites the
most famous resort is Cortina d'Ampezzo and there are many
other similar places among these spectacular peaks. All the
resorts are easy to reach, sometimes only a short car ride away
from the lakes, and they are much patronized by the local
inhabitants, especially at weekends. Life at the resorts is
cheerfully informal with après-ski parties and moonlight
sledge rides.

I'd like to join the class for beginners/for intermediate skiers.	**Vorrei unirmi ad una classe di sci per principianti/una classe a livello medio.**
Is there a beginner's slope?	**C'è una pista per principianti?**
Where can I hire skis?	**Dove posso affittare degli sci?**
a toboggan?	**un taboga?**
boots?	**degli scarponi?**
ski sticks?	**delle racchette?**
I have never skied before.	**Non ho mai sciato.**
These boots are uncomfortable.	**Questi scarponi sono scomodi.**
They are too tight/loose/big/small.	**Sono troppo stretti/larghi/grandi/piccoli.**
How far is the ski hoist from the hotel?	**Quant'è lontana la sciovia dall'albergo?**
Can I get a season ticket?	**Posso fare un abbonamento?**
Are the skiing conditions good this morning?	**È buona la neve oggi?**
Are all the pistes open?	**Sono aperte tutte le piste?**
Is there any cross-country skiing?	**Si può fare sci di fondo?**
Please help me up.	**Per favore, mi aiuti ad alzarmi.**
I think I've twisted my ankle.	**Penso di essermi slogato la caviglia.**
May I join the midnight sledge party?	**Posso partecipare al giro di mezzanotte in slitta?**

Sport

Two entrance tickets for the ice rink.	**Due biglietti d'ingresso per la pista di patinaggio.**
Is there a heated swimming pool?	**C'è un piscina riscaldata?**
Look out! I can't stop.	**Attenzione! Non posso fermarmi.**

VOCABULARY

avalanche	la valanga
cable car	la funivia
anorak	la giacca a vento
ice	il ghiaccio
ice skating	il pattinaggio sul ghiaccio
funicular	la funicolare
slalom	lo slalom
skates	i pattini
stem	lo stem
ski-lift	lo ski-lift
snow	la neve
toboggan run	la pista di toboga
waterproof trousers	i pantaloni impermeabili

General Services

If you are travelling independently or having a self-catering holiday at a villa or apartment, phrases for dealing with gas, electricity and plumbing problems will be indispensable. But even when all that is taken care of by someone else it is useful to be able to communicate with Post Office staff, telephone operators and other officials in their own language.

Post Office

Post Offices in Italy have the words **Posta e Telegrafo** outside them. Many of their mail boxes are painted red.

Where is the nearest post office?	**Dov'è il più vicino ufficio postale?**
What are the opening hours?	**A che ora è aperto?**
Can I cash an international money order here?	**È possibile incassare un vaglia postale internazionale qui?**
I want some stamps for a letter to Britain.	**Vorrei dei francobolli per una lettera per l'Inghilterra.**
What is the postcard postage rate for the USA?	**Quanto costa mandare una cartolina negli Stati Uniti?**
I'd like to register this letter.	**Vorrei fare questa lettera raccomandata.**
I want to send it airmail/express/surface/printed matter rate.	**Vorrei spedirla via aerea/espresso/per posta normale/come stampa.**
Where do I post parcels?	**Dove devo imbucare i pacchi?**
Do I need a customs form?	**Ho bisogno di un modulo per la dogana?**

General Services

Is there a poste restante here?	**C'è un fermo posta qui?**
Have you a letter for me?	**Ha nessuna lettera per me?**
May I have a telegram form?	**Mi può dare un modulo per telegrammi?**
I'll send it by the cheap rate/normal rate.	**Lo voglio mandare con la tariffa più economica/con la tariffa normale.**
When will it arrive?	**Quando arriverà?**
I want to make a local/international telephone call.	**Vorrei fare una telefonata locale/internazionale.**
Can you reverse the charges?	**Può addebitare la chiamata al ricevente?**
Switchboard, the line is engaged. Please try again later.	**Centralino, la linea è occupata. Provi di nuovo più tardi.**

The Police Station

I am a visitor to your country.	**Sono un(a) turista nel vostro paese.**
I would like to report a theft/loss/accident/crime.	**Vorrei denunciare un furto/una perdita/un incidente/un crimine.**
Someone has stolen my wallet.	**Qualcuno mi ha rubato il portafoglio.**
Something was stolen from my car/my hotel room.	**Mi hanno rubato qualcosa dalla macchina/dalla mia camera d'albergo.**
The theft occurred in the Via Roma at about four o'clock.	**Il furto è accaduto in via Roma circa alle quattro.**

136

I have lost my watch on the beach.	Ho perso il mio orologio sulla spiaggia.
It is valuable. It has sentimental value.	È un orologio di valore. Ha un valore sentimentale.
I will offer a reward.	Offrirò una ricompensa.
Someone has been knocked down.	Qualcuno è stato investito.
A lady has broken her leg.	Una signora si è rotta una gamba.
There is a man molesting women on the promenade.	C'è un uomo che molesta le donne al corso.
I have been swindled.	Sono stato imbrogliato.
Can a police officer come with me?	Un poliziotto può venire con me?
I will be a witness.	Farò da testimone.
I cannot be a witness. I did not see what was happening.	Non posso fare da testimone. Non ho visto cosa stava accadendo.
Is there anyone who speaks English?	C'è nessuno che parla inglese?

Electricity

The lights have gone out.	La luce è andata via.
The power plug is not working.	La spina non funziona.
The fuse has gone.	Il fusibile è saltato.
I think it is the switch.	Penso che sia l'interruttore.
There is a smell of burning.	C'è puzza di bruciato.
The stove won't light.	Il fornello non si accende.

General Services

The heating has broken down.	**Il riscaldamento si è rotto.**
Can you mend it straight away?	**Può aggiustarlo subito?**
Where is the fuse box?	**Dov'è la scatola dei fusibili?**
Which is the main switch?	**Qual'è l'interruttore principale?**

adaptor	**il trasformatore**
bulb	**la lampadina**
cooker	**la cucina**
electric fire	**la stufetta elettrica**
extensions lead	**la prolunga**
fuse wire	**il filo del fusibile**
hairdryer	**il phon**
insulating tape	**il nastro isolante**
iron	**il ferro da stiro**
plug	**la spina**
radio	**la radio**
razor point	**la presa per il rasoio**
refrigerator	**il frigorifero**
spotlight	**il proiettore**
television	**la televisione**
torch	**la lampadina tascabile**
water heater	**la stufa da bagno**

Gas

There is a smell of gas.	**C'è puzza di gas.**
It must be a gas leak.	**Ci deve essere una fuga.**
This is the gas meter.	**Questo è il contatore del gas.**

This gas jet won't light.	**Questo fornello non si accende.**
The pilot light isn't working.	**La spia non funziona.**
Is there any danger of an explosion?	**C'è pericolo di un'esplosione?**
I think the ventilator is blocked.	**Penso che il ventilatore sia bloccato.**
We can't get any hot water.	**Non riusciamo ad avere acqua calda.**

VOCABULARY

chimney	**il camino**
gaslight	**la luce a gas**
gaspipes	**i tubi del gas**
geyser	**la stufa da bagno a gas**
hammer	**il martello**
key	**la chiavetta**
lagging	**il materiale isolante**
monkey wrench	**la chiave inglese**
spanner	**la chiave a viti**
water heater	**lo scaldabagno**

Plumbing

Are you a plumber?	**Lei è l'idraulico?**
The sink is stopped up.	**Lo scarico del lavandino è otturato.**
There is a blockage in the pipe.	**C'è qualcosa nel tubo.**
The tap is dripping	**Il rubinetto perde.**

General Services

The tap needs a new washer.	**Il rubinetto ha bisogno di una nuova guarnizione.**
This water pipe is leaking.	**Questo tubo dell'acqua perde.**
The lavatory cistern won't fill.	**La cassetta del W.C. non si riempie.**
The valve is stuck.	**La valvola è bloccata.**
The float is punctured.	**Il galleggiante è bucato.**
The water tank has run dry.	**Il serbatoio dell'acqua è vuoto.**
The tank is overflowing.	**Il serbatoio dell'acqua trabocca.**

Vocabulary

basin	**il lavandino**
bath	**il bagno**
cesspool	**il pozzo nero**
immersion heater	**lo scaldabagno**
mains water	**l'acqua diretta**
main drainage	**la fogna centrale**
overflow pipe	**il tubo di scarico**
plug	**il tappo**

Personal Services

This section suggests useful phrases for such occasions as a visit to a doctor, dentist, hairdresser, hospital or beautician.

At the Doctor's

Can you recommend a good doctor?	Può consigliarmi un buon dottore?
Is there an English-speaking doctor in the area?	C'è un dottore che parli inglese nella zona?
Where is the surgery?	Dov'è la clinica?
I have an appointment. My name is ...	Ho un appuntamento. Il mio nome è ...
Can the doctor come to the hotel/house?	Il dottore può venire in albergo/a casa?
I'm not feeling well.	Non mi sento bene.
I feel sick/faint.	Mi sento male/svenire.
dizzy.	Ho le vertigini.
shivery.	Ho i brividi.
The pain is here.	Ho un dolore qui.
I have a temperature/headache/back ache/sore throat/sunburn.	Ho la febbre/mal di testa/mal di schiena/mal di gola/una scottatura da sole.
I have diarrhoea.	Ho la diarrea.
I have been like this since yesterday.	Mi sento così da ieri.
I have been vomiting.	Ho vomitato.
I am constipated.	Sono costipato(a).

Personal Services

I have hurt my . . .	**Mi sono fatto male a . . .**
Must I undress?	**Devo spogliarmi?**
Is it serious?	**È grave?**
Should I stay in bed?	**Devo stare a letto?**
Should I arrange to go home?	**È meglio tornare a casa?**
I am allergic to . . .	**Sono allergico(a) a . . .**
I have a heart condition.	**Ho dei disturbi al cuore.**
I am asthmatic/diabetic.	**Ho l'asma/il diabete.**
What attention do I get free under the national health arrangements?	**Quali cure sono gratis secondo gli accordi nazionali sanitari?**
Do I have to pay for hospitalization and medicines?	**Devo pagare ospedale e medicine?**
It's only a slight problem.	**È solo un piccolo problema.**

VOCABULARY

PARTS OF THE BODY

ankle	**la caviglia**
appendix	**l'appendice**
arm	**il braccio**
artery	**l'arteria**
back	**la schiena**
bladder	**la vescica**
blood	**il sangue**
bone	**l'osso**
bowels	**gli intestini**
breast	**il seno**
cheek	**la guancia**
chest	**il petto**

chin	**il mento**
collar bone	**la clavicola**
ear	**l'orecchio**
elbow	**il gomito**
eye	**l'occhio**
face	**la faccia**
finger	**il dito**
foot	**il piede**
forehead	**la fronte**
gland	**la ghiandola**
hand	**la mano**
heart	**il cuore**
heel	**il tallone**
hip	**l'anca**
intestine	**l'intestino**
jaw	**la mascella**
joint	**l'articolazione**
kidney	**il rene**
knee	**il ginocchio**
leg	**la gamba**
lip	**il labbro**
liver	**il fegato**
lung	**il polmone**
mouth	**la bocca**
muscle	**il muscolo**
neck	**il collo**
nerve	**il nervo**
nose	**il naso**
penis	**il pene**
rib	**la costola**
shoulder	**la spalla**
skin	**la pelle**
spine	**la spina dorsale**
stomach	**lo stomaco**
teeth	**i denti**
tendon	**il tendine**
testacle	**il testicolo**

thigh	**la coscia**
throat	**la gola**
thumb	**il pollice**
toe	**il dito del piede**
tongue	**la lingua**
tonsils	**le tonsille**
urine	**l'urina**
vein	**la vena**
vagina	**la vagina**
wrist	**il polso**
womb	**l'utero**

INDISPOSITIONS

blisters	**le vesciche**
dizziness	**il giramento di testa**
nausea	**la nausea**
shivers	**i brividi**
abcess	**l'ascesso**
asthma	**l'asma**
boil	**il foruncolo**
chill, cold	**il raffreddore**
convulsions	**le convulsioni**
cough	**la tosse**
cramp	**il crampo**
infection	**l'infezione**
diabetes	**il diabete**
diarrhoea	**la diarrea**
haemorrhoids	**le emorroidi**
hay fever	**la febbre da fieno**
indigestion	**l'indigestione**
inflammation	**l'infiammazione**
influenza	**l'influenza**
rhematism	**il reumatismo**
stiff neck	**il torcicollo**
sunstroke	**il colpo di sole**
tonsillitis	**la tonsillite**

ulcer	**l'ulcera**
whooping cough	**la tosse convulsa**
wound	**la ferita**

At the Dentist's

I need an appointment as soon as possible.	**Ho bisogno di un appuntamento il più presto possibile.**
I have a toothache/an abscess.	**Ho mal di denti/un ascesso.**
My gums are bleeding.	**Le mie gengive sanguinano.**
I have broken my dentures.	**Mi si è rotta la dentiera.**
Can you suggest a painkiller until I can see you?	**Che cosa posso prendere contro il dolore nel frattempo?**
The bad tooth is at the front/back/side.	**Il dente che mi fa male è davanti/dietro/da questa parte.**
Can you extract it?	**Me lo può togliere?**
Does it need a filling?	**Deve otturarmelo?**
Can you put in a temporary filling?	**Può mettermi un'otturazione provvisoria?**
Can I bite normally?	**Posso masticare normalmente?**
I'd prefer gas to an injection.	**Preferisco l'anestetico ad aria all'iniezione.**
What is your fee?	**Quant'è la sua parcella?**

At the Optician's

I have broken my glasses.	**Mi si sono rotti gli occhiali.**

145

Personal Services

Can you repair them temporarily?	Può aggiustarli temporaneamente?
The lens is broken. Can you get a new one quickly?	La lente è rotta. Potete sostituirla velocemente?
Have you got contact lenses?	Vendete lenti a contatto?
I'd like a pair of tinted spectacles.	Vorrei un paio di occhiali colorati.
Do you sell binoculars/a magnifying glass/sunglasses?	Vendete binocoli/una lente d'ingrandimento/occhiali da sole?
I had better have an eye test.	Vorrei fare l'esame della vista.
I am shortsighted/long sighted.	Sono miope/presbite.
How long will it take to make me some new glasses?	Quanto tempo dovrò aspettare per avere un nuovo paio di occhiali?
How much will they cost?	Quanto costeranno?

At the Chiropodist's

I have a painful corn.	Ho un callo che mi fa male.
Can you remove it?	Può togliermelo?
My bunion is rubbing against my shoe.	Questo callo urta la scarpa.
I have a hard spot on the ball of my foot.	Ho un durone sul polpastrello del piede.
My nails need attention. One of them is ingrowing.	Mi guardi le unghie. Una si sta incarnendo.
Have you anything to soften them?	Ha niente per renderle più morbide?
I have stubbed my toe.	Ho urtato il dito del piede.

The soles of my feet are very sore.	**Le piante dei piedi mi fanno male.**

At the Hairdresser's

Where is the nearest hairdresser? Is there one in the hotel?	**Dov'è il parrucchiere più vicino? Ce n'è uno nell'albergo?**
I'd like to make an appointment.	**Vorrei avere un appuntamento.**
I'd like a shampoo and set.	**Vorrei uno shampoo e messa in piega.**
I want it cut and set.	**Li voglio tagliati e messi in piega.**
I wear it brushed forward with a fringe.	**Li porto spazzolati in avanti con una frangetta.**
I like it brushed back.	**Mi piacciono spazzolati indietro.**
Can you put some waves/curls in?	**Può farli ondulati/ricci?**
Can you draw it back into a bun?	**Può farmi una crocchia?**
Can you give me a colour rinse?	**Può farmi un colorante?**
I think I will have it dyed.	**Penso che li tingerò.**
Have you got a colour chart?	**Ha un campione dei colori?**
No hairspray, thank you.	**Niente lacca per capelli, per favore.**
I'd like a manicure.	**Vorrei la manicure.**
What is the name of this varnish?	**Qual'è il nome di questo smalto?**

Personal Services

auburn	**castano**
blonde	**biondo**
brunette	**bruno**
comb	**il pettine**
dryer	**il phon/il casco**
hairnet	**la retina**
hairpiece	**il toupet**
hair pin	**la forcella**
scissors	**le forbici**
razor	**il rasoio**
rollers	**i bigodini**
styling	**l'acconciatura**

At the Beauty Salon

I'd like a complete beauty treatment/just a facial, please.	**Vorrei un trattamento completo/solo il viso, per favore.**
I'd like to change my make-up.	**Vorrei cambiare il mio trucco.**
I'd like something more suitable for the seaside.	**Vorrei qualcosa di più pratico per le vacanze al mare.**
something lighter in tone.	**qualcosa con toni più leggeri.**
a more open-air look. something for the evening.	**un trucco acqua e sapone. un trucco da sera.**
I have a delicate skin.	**Ho una pelle delicata.**
Can you please suggest a new eye make-up?	**Mi può consigliare un trucco per gli occhi differente?**

148

I think that is too heavy.	**Penso che questo sia troppo pesante.**
Have you any false eyelashes?	**Ha delle ciglia finte?**
I think my eyebrows need plucking.	**Credo di dover depilare le sopracciglia.**
I'd like to see some new lipstick colours.	**Vorrei vedere i nuovi colori di rossetto.**

At the Laundry/Cleaner's

I'd like them washed and pressed, please.	**Li vorrei lavati e stirati, per favore.**
Will you iron the shirts?	**Stirate le camicie?**
I will collect them tomorrow.	**Passerò a prenderle domani.**
Do you deliver?	**Le mandate a casa?**
Do you do mending?	**Fate riparazioni?**
This tear needs patching.	**Questo strappo deve essere rammendato.**
Can you sew this button on?	**Può attaccarmi questo bottone?**
Will this stain come out?	**Verrà via questa macchia?**
It is coffee/blood/grease/biro.	**È di caffè/di sangue/di grasso/di biro.**
Can you mend this invisibly?	**Può farmi un rammendo invisibile?**
This blouse/coat/dress is not mine.	**Questa camicetta/questo cappotto/vestito non è mia(o).**
My trousers are missing.	**Mancano i miei pantaloni.**

Personal Services

This was not torn when I brought it to you.	**Questo non era strappato quando ve l'ho portato.**
How long does the launderette stay open?	**Fino a quando è aperta la lavanderia?**

Vocabulary

bleach	**la varechina**
cleaning fluid	**il liquido per pulire**
clothes hanger	**l'attaccapanni**
cold/hot/warm water	**l'acqua fredda/calda/tiepida**
the dryer	**l'essiccatoio**
launderette	**la lavanderia**
rinse	**il risciacquo**
soap powder	**il sapone in polvere**
washing machine	**la lavatrice**

At the Men's Hairdresser's

I want a haircut, please.	**Vorrei un taglio di capelli, per favore.**
Just a trim. I haven't much time.	**Vorrei spuntarli solamente. Non ho molto tempo.**
Please give me a shampoo.	**Mi faccia uno shampoo, per favore.**
I would like it cut shorter.	**Li vorrei tagliati corti.**
Leave it long.	**Li lasci lunghi.**
You are taking too much off.	**Ne sta tagliando troppi.**
Take a little more off the back/sides/top.	**Me li tagli un pò di più di dietro/di lato/in cima.**

I part my hair on the left/right.	**Porto la riga a sinistra/a destra.**
I'd like an alcohol rub/a singe.	**Vorrei una frizione alcoolica/bruciare le punte.**
Please give me a shave.	**Mi faccia la barba, per favore.**
Please trim my beard/moustache/sideboards.	**Mi spunti la barba/i baffi/le basette, per favore.**
No thank you, I do not want a facial massage.	**No, grazie, non desidero un massaggio facciale.**
I will have a manicure.	**Vorrei fare la manicure.**
May I have a hand towel?	**Potrei avere un asciugamano?**
Put some eau de cologne on but no cream.	**Ci metta pure l'acqua di Colonia, ma niente crema.**
Move the mirror a bit more to the right.	**Sposti lo specchio più a destra.**
Yes, that's fine.	**Sì, va bene così.**

Making Friends

Good morning/good afternoon/good evening.	**Buon giorno/buona sera/buona sera.**
May I introduce myself/my friend John/my wife?	**Posso presentarmi/presentarle il mio amico John/mia moglie?**
My name is ...	**Mi chiamo ...**
How do you do?	**Piacere.**
Are you staying at this hotel/at this resort?	**Soggiorna in questo albergo/in questo paese?**
Are you enjoying your holiday?	**Sta passando delle buone vacanze?**
How long have you been on holiday?	**È molto che è in vacanza?**
Do you always come here?	**Viene sempre qui?**
I'd like you to meet my friend ...	**Vorrei presentarle i miei amici ...**
Would you care to have a drink with us?	**Prende qualcosa da bere con noi?**
What would you like?	**Che cosa prende?**
Please, I insist that you let me pay.	**Insisto per pagare.**
I'm afraid that I don't speak Italian very well.	**Mi dispiace di non parlare italiano molto bene.**
It is very nice to talk to an Italian person.	**È un piacere parlare ad un Italiano.**
Which part of Italy do you come from?	**Da che parte d'Italia viene?**

Making Friends

I am here with my wife/my husband/family/friends.	**Sono qui con mia moglie/mio marito/la mia famiglia/i miei amici.**
Are you alone?	**È solo(a)?**
We come from Manchester/England.	**Veniamo da Manchester/dall'Inghilterra.**
Have you been to England?	**È mai stato(a) in Inghilterra?**
If you come, please let me know.	**Mi faccia sapere se viene.**
This is my address.	**Questo è il mio indirizzo.**
I hope to see you again soon.	**Spero di rivederla presto.**
Perhaps you would like to meet for a drink after dinner?	**Pensa che ci possiamo vedere dopo cena per andare a bere qualcosa?**
I would like to very much.	**Mi piacerebbe molto.**
At what time shall I come?	**A che ora posso venire?**
Have you got a family?	**Ha famiglia?**
Would you like to see some photos of our house and our children?	**Le piacerebbe vedere alcune foto di casa nostra e dei bambini?**
Are you going to the gala?	**Va alla serata di gala?**
Would you like to make up a party?	**Le piacerebbe formare una compagnia?**
It has been so very nice to meet you.	**È stato un piacere conoscerla.**
You have been very kind.	**È stata veramente gentile.**

Dating Someone

Are you on holiday?	È qui in vacanza?
Do you live here?	Vive qui?
Do you like this place?	Le piace questo posto?
I've just arrived.	Sono appena arrivato(a).
What is there to do?	Che cosa c'è da fare?
I don't know anyone here.	Non conosco nessuno qui.
I'm with a group of students.	Sono con un gruppo di studenti.
I'm travelling alone.	Viaggio da solo(a).
I'm on my way round Europe.	Sto facendo il giro d'Europa.
I come from Scotland/Australia/New Zealand.	Vengo dalla Scozia/dall'Australia/dalla Nuova Zelanda.
Do you mind if I try my Italian on you?	Le dispiace se provo il mio italiano con Lei?
My Italian is not very good.	Il mio italiano non è molto buono.
Would you like a drink?	Vuole qualcosa da bere?
What are you doing this evening?	Che cosa fa stasera?
Would you like to go to a discotheque/join our party?	Le piacerebbe andare in una discoteca/unirsi a noi?
Do you like dancing/concerts/opera?	Le piace ballare/le piacciono i concerti/l'opera?
Can I walk along with you?	Posso accompagnarla?
Which way are you going?	Da che parte va?

155

Making Friends

Do you mind if I sit here?	**Le dispiace se mi siedo qui?**
This is my friend, Tom.	**Questo è il mio amico Tom.**
Do you have a girl friend?	**Ha un'amica?**
We could make a foursome.	**Potremmo fare un quartetto.**
Do you play tennis/golf?	**Gioca a tennis/a golf?**
Do you go swimming?	**Nuota?**
Which beach do you go to?	**A quale spiaggia va?**
Would you like to come for a drive/a boat ride?	**Le piacerebbe fare un giro in macchina/in barca?**
It would be nice if you would.	**Sarebbe molto bello se accettasse.**
Thanks for coming out with me.	**Grazie per esser uscita con me.**
I enjoyed it.	**Mi sono divertito(a).**
Can we meet again?	**Ci possiamo vedere ancora?**
How about tomorrow?	**Che ne dice di domani?**
No thanks, I'm busy.	**No grazie, sono occupato(a).**
Please stop bothering me.	**La smetta di importunarmi.**

Mutual Interest

Do you play cards?	**Gioca a carte?**
Would you like to make a four at bridge?	**Le piacerebbe fare il quarto (la quarta) a bridge?**
We play canasta/poker/rummy.	**Giochiamo a canasta/a poker/a ramino.**
It is an English game.	**È un gioco inglese.**
Are you a chess player?	**Gioca a scacchi?**

I'll ask the concierge if the hotel has a chess board.	**Chiederò al portiere se c'è una scacchiera in albergo.**
This is your king/queen/knight/ bishop/castle/pawn.	**Questo è il suo re/la sua regina/il suo cavallo/il suo alfiere/la sua torre/il suo pedone.**
Do you play draughts or dominoes?	**Gioca a dama o a domino?**
There is table tennis in the hotel. Would you care for a game?	**C'è il ping-pong nell'albergo. Le va una partita?**
Do you read English?	**Sa leggere in inglese?**
Would you like to borrow this book/newspaper?	**Vuole prendere in prestito questo libro/giornale?**

Conversations

There are certain universal subjects of conversation which provide a bridge for communication with strangers all over the world. Among these are the weather, families, home, the cost of living and pets.

The following conversational phrases are designed to start you on an acquaintanceship with people who do not speak English.

About the Weather

It is a fine day.	È una bella giornata.
It's not a very nice day.	Non è una giornata molto bella.
Will it rain all day/later/ tomorrow, do you think?	Pensa che pioverà tutto il giorno/piu tardi/domani?
It's going to be hot/cold today.	Farà caldo/freddo oggi.
It's rather windy.	È piuttosto ventoso.
I think there is a thunderstorm coming.	Penso che ci sia un temporale in arrivo.
Look at the lightning.	Guardi che lampi.
It will soon clear up.	Schiarirà presto.
We don't get this kind of weather at home.	Non abbiamo questo tipo di tempo a casa.
It's a pity it is so dull.	È un peccato che sia così grigio.
Did you see the beautiful sunrise/sunset?	Ha visto che meravigliosa alba/che meraviglioso tramonto?

We had a very good/very poor summer last year.	L'anno scorso abbiamo avuto una bellissima/bruttissima estate.
There's a lot of haze about today.	C'è molta foschia oggi.
The atmosphere is very clear.	L'aria è molto limpida.
Is it cold here in the winter?	Fa freddo qui in inverno?
I love the spring/summer/autumn.	Mi piace la primavera/l'estate/l'autunno.
What does the barometer say?	Che cosa dice il barometro?

VOCABULARY

breeze	la brezza
cloudburst	l'acquazzone
cloudy	nuvoloso
drizzle	la pioggerella
dry	secco
forecast	le previsioni del tempo
hail	la grandine
meteorological office	l'ufficio meteorologico
mist	la nebbia
pressure	la pressione
rain	la pioggia
sleet	il nevischio
snow	la neve
sunny	soleggiato
temperature	la temperatura
weather report	il bollettino meteorologico
wet	umido

About Families

This is my wife/husband/daughter/son.	**Questa è mia moglie/mio marito/mia figlia/mio figlio.**
My son is an architect/doctor/student/teacher/engineer.	**Mio figlio è architetto/medico/studente/insegnante/ingegnere.**
My daughter is at school.	**Mia figlia studia.**
She is taking her examinations.	**Sta facendo gli esami.**
Then she will go to university/art school/teacher's training college.	**Poi andrà all'Università/all'Accademia artistica/a un corso di specializzazione per insegnanti.**
She learnt some Italian at school.	**Ha imparato un pò di italiano a scuola.**
My wife is Scottish, but her mother is Italian.	**Mia moglie è Scozzese, ma sua madre è Italiana.**
My father was a teacher.	**Mio padre era un insegnante.**
The children prefer to have holidays on their own.	**I ragazzi preferiscono fare le vacanze da soli.**
They prefer camping.	**Preferiscono fare il campeggio.**
My eldest/youngest son/daughter is married and lives in ...	**Il mio figlio/la mia figlia più grande/più giovane è sposato(a) e vive in ...**
Would you like to see some photos of our family?	**Vuole vedere le foto della nostra famiglia?**
The younger children stayed at home with their grandparents.	**I figli più piccoli sono restati a casa con i nonni.**
Are these your children?	**Sono questi i suoi figli?**

The boy/girl looks like his/her mother/father.	**Il ragazzo/la ragazza assomiglia a sua madre/a suo padre.**
How old is he/she?	**Quanti anni ha lui/lei?**
My daughter is fourteen.	**Mia figlia ha quattordici anni.**

VOCABULARY

birthday	**il compleanno**
aunt	**la zia**
cousin	**il cugino**
divorce	**il divorzio**
mother-in-law	**la suocera**
marriage	**il matrimonio**
relatives	**i parenti**
uncle	**lo zio**
wedding	**lo sposalizio**

About Homes

We have a house in town/in the country.	**Abbiamo una casa in città/in campagna.**
It is a two-storey house. a detached house/a semi-detached house.	**È una villetta a due piani. una casa separata dalle altre/separata solo da una parte.**
a cottage. a maisonette.	**un cottage. un appartamento su due piani.**
a flat.	**un appartamento.**
We have a large garden/a patio.	**Abbiamo un grande giardino/un patio.**

161

There are two living rooms. One has a French window, the other a bay window.	Ci sono due soggiorni. Uno ha una vetrata, l'altro una finestra bombata.
There is a fireplace in the dining room.	C'è un camino nella sala da pranzo.
The house is centrally heated/has air conditioning.	La casa ha il riscaldamento centrale/l'aria condizionata.
We have two garages.	Abbiamo due garages.
The back garden has a lawn and swimming pool.	Nel giardino sul retro c'è un prato e una piscina.
In our village there are many old houses.	Nel nostro villaggio ci sono molte case vecchie.
We prefer a modern house.	Preferiamo una casa moderna.
What kind of house have you got?	Che tipo di casa avete?
I like Italian-style houses.	Mi piacciono le case di stile italiano.
Do you cook by gas or electricity?	Usate la cucina a gas o elettrica?
In a warm climate tiled floors are delightful.	Con un clima caldo i pavimenti di mattonelle sono deliziosi.
Wall-to-wall carpeting makes a house warm in winter.	Le moquettes fanno la casa calda in inverno.
Built-in cupboards make a room seem larger.	Gli armadi a muro fanno sembrare le camere più spaziose.
Old furniture is lovely but very expensive.	I mobili antichi sono belli ma costosi.

VOCABULARY

balcony	il balcone
brick	il mattone
ceiling	il soffitto
chimney	il camino
door	la porta
drains	la fognatura
foundations	le fondamenta
gable	il comignolo
mains electricity	l'impianto elettrico centrale
mains gas	l'impianto del gas centrale
plumbing	il sistema idraulico
roof	il tetto
stone	la pietra
terrace	la terrazza
thatch	la paglia
tiles	le mattonelle
wall	la parete
window	la finestra
window frame	l'intelaiatura della finestra
window pane	il vetro della finestra
wood	il legno

On Business

I have an appointment with the manager.	Ho un appuntamento col direttore.
I am from Smith and Company.	Sono della Smith and Company.
Here is my card.	Ecco il mio biglietto da visita.
It is good of you to see me.	È gentile da parte vostra ricevermi.

May I show you our catalogue/samples?	**Posso mostrarle il nostro catalogo/i nostri campioni?**
My company manufactures knitwear.	**La mia società produce maglieria.**
We are looking for agents.	**Stiamo cercando agenti.**
Our wholesale prices/retail prices are on this list.	**I nostri prezzi all'ingrosso/prezzi al dettaglio sono su questa lista.**
There is a special discount for a large quantity.	**C'è una riduzione speciale per ordinazioni in blocco.**
Delivery is within two months/immediate.	**La consegna è nel giro di due mesi/immediata.**
The prices are f.o.b.	**I prezzi sono fob.**
I would like to see your products.	**Vorrei vedere i vostri prodotti.**
Have you a showroom in the town?	**Avete una sala d'esposizione in città?**
What are your terms of business?	**Quali sono le vostre condizioni?**
Do you already have agents in my country?	**Avete già agenti nel mio paese?**
Can you make modifications to this model?	**Può fare delle modifiche a questo modello?**
May I take some samples with me?	**Posso tenermi alcuni campioni?**
I will give you an order now.	**Faccio un'ordinazione adesso.**
Can you look after the packing and shipping?	**Può occuparsi dell'imballaggio e della spedizione per nave?**

There is only a small market for these goods.

Il mercato è ristretto per questi prodotti.

VOCABULARY

banker	il banchiere
balance sheet	il bilancio
bill	la fattura
bill of exchange	la cambiale
clerk	l'impiegato
credit	il credito
contract	il contratto
correspondence	la corrispondenza
certificate	il certificato
draft	la tratta
debit	il debito
export	l'esportazione
freight	il trasporto
insurance	l'assicurazione
import	l'importazione
invoice	la fattura
merchant	il commerciante
receipt	la ricevuta
remittance	il pagamento
sale	la vendita
warehouse	il magazzino

Looking after your Money

The Bank

Where is the nearest bank?	**Dov'è la banca più vicina?**
Do you accept travellers' cheques at this bank?	**Posso incassare assegni turistici in questa banca?**
Can I use a Eurocheque card?	**Posso usare la carta assegni Eurocheque?**
Do you issue money against a credit card?	**Anticipate denaro su una carta di credito?**
I am expecting a remittance.	**Sto aspettando una rimessa.**
I have a letter of credit.	**Ho una lettera di credito.**
I would like a draft to send away.	**Vorrei un assegno circolare da spedire.**
What is the rate of exchange for the pound/dollar/Australian dollar?	**Qual'è il tasso di cambio per la sterlina/il dollaro/il dollaro australiano?**
What is your commission charge?	**Quant'è la vostra commissione?**
I will have it all in 500 lire notes.	**Vorrei il tutto in biglietti da cinquecento lire.**
Please give me 10,000 lire worth of change.	**Per favore, mi dia dieci mila lire in spiccioli.**
Can you split this cheque into several currencies?	**Posso incassare quest'assegno in più valute diverse?**

Money Matters

I will have some German marks, Swiss francs and Italian lire.	**Vorrei marchi tedeschi, franchi svizzeri e lire italiane.**
Can I open a temporary bank account?	**Posso aprire un conto provvisorio?**
Can you arrange for some money to be sent from my bank in Britain?	**Può chiedere alla mia banca in Gran Bretagna di mandare dei soldi?**
I seem to be 100 lire short. Can you please count it again?	**Mi sembra di avere cento lire in meno. Può contarli di nuovo, per favore?**
Have you a card showing current exchange rates?	**Ha una lista dei tassi di cambio?**

VOCABULARY

Bank of England	**la Banca d'Inghilterra**
cashier	**il cassiere/la cassiera**
cheque book	**il libretto d'assegni**
credit	**il credito**
coins	**le monete**
deposit slip	**il modulo di deposito**
debit	**il debito**
foreign exchange regulations	**le disposizioni dell'ufficio cambi**
manager	**il direttore**
notes	**le banconote**
treasury	**il ministero del Tesoro**
signature	**la firma**

Bureau de Change

Are you open outside banking hours?	**Siete aperti fuori orario di sportello?**
Does the rate of exchange alter outside normal hours?	**Il vostro tasso di cambio varia fuori orario?**
Are you open on Sundays?	**Siete aperti di domenica?**
Can you show me your rates of exchange?	**Può mostrarmi i vostri tassi di cambio?**
Do you give the same rate for notes as for travellers' cheques?	**I tassi per le banconote sono gli stessi che per gli assegni turistici?**

On Losing Travellers' Cheques or Credit Cards

When this happens you should immediately notify the company that has issued the cheques or card, but you may need help from a local hotelier or banker.

I have lost my travellers' cheques/credit card.	**Ho perduto i miei assegni turistici/la mia carta di credito.**
May I ask them to communicate with me through you?	**Posso chiedere che loro comunichino tramite voi?**
Have you a British representative?	**Avete un ufficio di rappresentanza in Gran Bretagna?**
I hope they will be able to refund the cheques quickly. I have no other money.	**Spero che possano rifondermi presto gli assegni. Non ho più soldi.**
I will ask my bank at home to send some money to you.	**Chiederò alla mia banca di mandarvi dei soldi.**

Will you accept a British cheque in payment of the hotel bill?

Accettate un assegno inglese in pagamento del conto dell'albergo?

Reference Section

Numbers

1	uno	29	ventinove
2	due	30	trenta
3	tre	31	trentuno
4	quattro	32	trentadue
5	cinque	33	trentatre
6	sei	34	trentaquattro
7	sette	35	trentacinque
8	otto	36	trentasei
9	nove	37	trentasette
10	dieci	38	trentotto
11	undici	39	trentanove
12	dodici	40	quaranta
13	tredici	50	cinquanta
14	quattordici	60	sessanta
15	quindici	70	settanta
16	sedici	80	ottanta
17	diciassette	90	novanta
18	diciotto	100	cento
19	diciannove	101	centouno
20	venti	110	centodieci
21	ventuno	200	duecento
22	ventidue	1000	mille
23	ventitre	1001	mille e uno
24	ventiquattro	1100	mille e cento
24	venticinque	2000	duemila
26	ventisei	1,000,000	un milione
27	ventisette	1,000,000,000	un miliardo
28	ventotto		

first	**primo**	once	**una volta**
second	**secondo**	twice	**due volte**
third	**terzo**	three times	**tre volte**
fourth	**quarto**	half	**mezzo**
fifth	**quinto**	quarter	**un quarto**
sixth	**sesto**	third	**un terzo**
seventh	**settimo**	eighth	**un ottavo**
eighth	**ottavo**	a pair of	**un paio di**
ninth	**nono**	a dozen	**una dozzina**
tenth	**decimo**		

Time

Greenwich Mean Time	**L'orario ufficiale di Greenwich**
Central European Time	**L'orario dell'Europa centrale**
Atlantic Time	**L'orario atlantico**
Date line	**La linea del cambiamento di data**
AM/PM	**di mattina/di sera**
24-hour clock	**l'orologio ventiquattro ore**
summer time	**l'ora legale**
it is 12.15/12.20/12.30/12.35/ 12.45/1.00	**sono le dodici e un quarto/le dodici e venti/le dodici e mezzo/le dodici e trentacinque/è l'una meno quarto/ è l'una.**
midnight, midday.	**mezzanotte, mezzogiorno.**

Phrases Referring to Time

What time is it?	**Che ora è?**
It is late.	**È tardi.**
It is early.	**È presto.**
Are we on time?	**Siamo puntuali?**
At what time shall we meet?	**A che ora ci incontriamo?**
At what time are we expected?	**A che ora ci aspettano?**
On the hour.	**Ogni ora in punto.**

Reference Section

By the minute.	**Ogni minuto.**
Every second.	**Ogni secondo.**
At regular intervals.	**Ad intervalli regolari.**
Day by day.	**Giorno per giorno.**

VOCABULARY

days	**giorni**
weeks	**settimane**
years	**anni**
Sunday	**domenica**
Monday	**lunedì**
Tuesday	**martedì**
Wednesday	**mercoledì**
Thursday	**giovedì**
Friday	**venerdì**
Saturday	**sabato**
daybreak	**l'aurora**
dawn	**l'alba**
morning	**il mattino**
afternoon	**il pomeriggio**
evening	**la sera**
night	**la notte**
today	**oggi**
yesterday	**ieri**
tomorrow	**domani**
the day before yesterday	**l'altroieri**
two days ago	**due giorni fa**
the day after tomorrow	**dopodomani**
the following day	**il giorno seguente**
weekday	**il giorno lavorativo**
a day off	**un giorno di permesso**
birthday	**compleanno**
Christmas Day	**Natale**

New Year's Day	**Capodanno**
All Saint's Day	**Ognissanti**
May day	**la festa del lavoro**
weekend	**fine settimana**
last week	**la settimana scorsa**
next week	**la settimana prossima**
for two weeks	**per due settimane**
January	**gennaio**
February	**febbraio**
March	**marzo**
April	**aprile**
May	**maggio**
June	**giugno**
July	**luglio**
August	**agosto**
September	**settembre**
October	**ottobre**
November	**novembre**
December	**dicembre**
calendar month	**mese secondo il calendario**
lunar month	**mese lunare**
monthly	**mensilmente**
since January	**da gennaio**
last month	**il mese scorso**
next month	**il mese prossimo**
the month before	**il mese prima**
the first of the month	**il primo del mese**
the first of March	**il primo di marzo**
years	**gli anni**
BC	**AC**
AD	**DC**
Leap year	**anno bisestile**

Seasons and Weather

spring, summer, autumn, winter.	**primavera, estate, autunno, inverno.**
Equinox, Midsummer, Solstice, Midwinter.	**Equinozio, mezza estate, solstizio, nel mezzo dell'inverno.**
In spring time it is fresh.	**In primavera fa fresco.**
In summer it is hot.	**D'estate fa caldo.**
In autumn it is cool.	**In autunno fa fresco.**
In winter it is cold.	**D'inverno fa freddo.**

Temperature Equivalents

FAHRENHEIT		CENTIGRADE
212	Boiling point	100
100		37·8
98·4	Body temperature	37
86		30
77		25
68		20
50		10
32	Freezing point	0
0		−18

To convert Fahrenheit to Centigrade subtract 32 and divide by 1·8.

To convert Centigrade to Fahrenheit multiply by 1·8 and add 32.

Pressure

The barometer tells you the air pressure of the atmosphere: 15 lb. per sq. in. is normal air pressure at sea level. This equals 1·1 kg. per sq. cm.

A tyre gauge tells you the pressure of your car tyres.

POUNDS PER SQUARE INCH	KILOGRAMS PER SQUARE CENTIMETRE
16	1·12
18	1·27
20	1·41
22	1·55
24	1·69
26	1·83
28	1·97

177

Measurements of Distance

One kilometre = 1000 metres = 0·62 miles

One hundred centimetres = 1 metre = 3·3 ft.

One centimetre = 0·39 inches.

The following table gives equivalents for metres and feet. The figure in the centre column can stand for either feet or metres and the equivalent should then be read off in the appropriate column.

METRES	METRES AND FEET	FEET
0·30	1	3·28
0·61	2	6·56
0·91	3	9·84
1·22	4	13·12
1·52	5	16·40
1·83	6	19·68
2·13	7	22·97
2·44	8	26·25
2·74	9	29·53
3·05	10	32·81
3·35	11	36·09
3·66	12	39·37
3·96	13	42·65
4·27	14	45·93
4·57	15	49·21
4·88	16	52·49
5·18	17	55·77
5·49	18	59·05
5·79	19	62·34
6·10	20	65·62
7·62	25	82·02
15·24	50	164·04
22·86	75	264·06
30·48	100	328·08

MILES	MILES AND KILOMETRES	KILOMETRES
0·62	1	1·61
1·24	2	3·22
1·86	3	4·82
2·49	4	6·44
3·11	5	8·05
3·73	6	9·66
4·35	7	11·27
4·97	8	12·88
5·59	9	14·48
6·21	10	16·09
15·53	25	40·23
31·07	50	80·47
46·60	75	120·70
62·14	100	160·93

For motorists it is useful to remember that

30 miles is 48·3 km.
70 miles is 112·7 km.
but
70 km. is 43·75 miles
100 km. is 62·50 miles

To convert kilometres to miles, divide by 8 and multiply by 5.

To convert miles to kilometres, divide by 5 and multiply by 8.

Measurements of Quantity

Weight

POUNDS	POUNDS AND KILOGRAMS	KILOGRAMS
2·20	1	0·45
4·40	2	0·90
6·61	3	1·36
8·81	4	1·81
11·02	5	2·27
13·23	6	2·72
15·43	7	3·18
17·64	8	3·63

OUNCES	GRAMS
0·5	14·12
1	28·35
2	56·70
3	85·05
4	113·40
5	141·75
6	170·10
7	198·45
8 (½ lb)	226·80
12	340·19
16 (1 lb.)	453·59

One kilogram = 1000 grams = 2·2 lb.

Half a kilogram = 500 grams = 1·1 lb.

When shopping for small items, it is useful to remember that 100 grams is about 3½ oz.

One metric ton is 1000 kilograms.

Liquid Measures

U.K. Pints	U.K. Pints and Litres	Litres
1·76	1	0·57
3·52	2 (1 quart)	1·14
5·28	3	1·70
7·04	4	2·27
8·80	5	2·84
10·56	6	3·41
12·32	7	3·98
14·08	8 (1 gallon)	4·55
15·84	9	5·11
17·60	10	5·68

1 litre = 1·76 pints

One tenth of a litre is a decilitre or 0·18 of a pint.

One hundredth of a litre is a centilitre or 0·018 of a pint.

One hundred litres are a hectolitre or 22 gallons.

One gallon = 4·6 litres.

One quart = 1·14 litres.

One pint = 0·57 litres.

Clothing Sizes

Measurements for clothes are measured according to the
metric system in Italy. Here are the equivalent sizes for the
main articles of clothing:

Women

DRESSES AND COATS

British	34	36	38	40	42	44	46
American	32	34	36	38	40	42	44
Continental	40	42	44	46	48	50	52

Men

SUITS

British and American	36	38	40	42	44	46
Continental	46	48	50	52	54	56

SHIRTS

British and American	14	14½	15	15½	16	16½	17
Continental	36	37	38	39	41	42	43

Index

183